KING DAVID
AND I

KING DAVID AND I

Bob Buess

Price $1.95
Send 60¢ postage for the first three books ordered by mail.
Add 5¢ for each additional book.
Texas residents include 4% sales tax.
Individuals may deduct a 35% discount in orders of 30 books or more. Texas residents please include sales tax after the discount is figured.

Order books from
Bob Buess
Box 959
Van, Texas 75790

Copyright © 1980 by Bob Buess
Printed in the United States of America

ISBN: 0-934244-09-X

INTRODUCTION

The believer is seated with Christ in heavenly places. He is a king under Jesus Christ. Every believer is to represent Jesus in a very definite way.

King David was symbolic of the real throne that Jesus established. Jesus is now seated on David's throne. As a believer you are seated with Jesus on this throne. You are to believe like a king.

The great anointing that was on David was shared by his men. You share with Jesus His anointing. His exploits are your exploits.

All of the basic victories in David's life passed on to his men and to subsequent kings as they submitted to them. Jesus has given you power over all the power of the enemy.

See yourself ruling from the throne of Jesus, your David. Never come down under your problem and feel sorry for yourself. Take authority over the situation as a king.

The reigning you do on this throne is by the power of God. This power is creative. As you learn to flow with the throne principles, you will actually learn to create by the energy of the power of God. This will not be the flesh. "It is the spirit that quickeneth."

The ultimate purpose of reigning is to bless others and to bring glory to God as your ministry comes into fuller blossom.

Many doors that are now closed to your ministry will be opened by your knowledge of the throne principles.

Praise is the force that destroys the negative forces in your life.

CONTENTS

CHAPTER 1
The Law of the Throne................1

CHAPTER 2
David's Throne Is Symbolic
 of Life in Christ...................8

CHAPTER 3
Reigning From the Throne.............42

CHAPTER 4
Reigning by the Power of God..........64

CHAPTER 5
The Value of Obedience in Reigning.....86

CHAPTER 6
Waiting on God —
 A Prerequisite to Reigning............99

CHAPTER 7
Reigning by Stepping
  Through Open Doors.................112

CHAPTER 8
Reigning by Praising...................125

CHAPTER 1

THE LAW OF THE THRONE

VISUALIZE YOURSELF ON THE THRONE WITH JESUS

Ephesians 2:5-6 "Even when we were dead in sins, hath quickened us together with Christ... and hath raised us up together, and made us to sit together in heavenly places in Christ Jesus."

Instead of seeing yourself from the position of your problems and frustrations, see yourself from the vantage point of the throne of Jesus and walk through your problems. See yourself on His throne and bring into existence a greater ministry. Bring in more finances for your ministry, business, or whatever. Get a better job. Reign from that throne. Believe from His throne. Act like a king.

VISUALIZE YOURSELF AS A KING

Revelation 1:6 "And hath made us kings and priests unto God and his father..."

Jesus is king.
You are one with Him.
You are joined to Him.
He is in you.
You are a king. See yourself as a king in every situation. See this king-ministry promoting you. Stop and visualize King Jesus shining out through your life. Problems that once seemed insurmountable will begin to diminish. Move with authority. Think with Jesus' authority. Release this king-ministry. It is stored up in you. Jesus Christ in you is that king. The Messiah lives in you. Galatians 2:20: "... Not I, but Christ liveth in me..."

YOU ARE SEATED WITH CHRIST ON DAVID'S THRONE

Luke 1:32 "... The Lord God shall give unto him the throne of his father David."

Acts 13:34 "... I will give you the sure mercies of David."

(RV: *"I will give you the holy and sure blessings of David."* Diaglott: *"I will give you the holy things of David the faithful."*)

John 7:42 "... Christ cometh of the seed of David..."

Acts 15:16-17 "After this I will return,

and will build again the tabernacle of David, which is fallen down ... that the residue of men might seek the Lord, and all the Gentiles, upon whom my name is called ..."

Jesus is the real David of prophecy. David, speaking of the prophecies given to him about his kingdom and his sons, said, *"Thou hast also spoken of thy servant's house for a great while to come ..."* 1 Chronicles 17:17.

"The Lord shall give unto him the throne of his father David."

Throughout the Old Testament David's throne is spoken of in a prophetic way. Jesus is the fulfillment of that prophecy. Everything good that happened on David's throne was prophetic of the reign of Jesus through the church.

1 Chronicles 17:11-17 "It shall come to pass when thy days be expired that thou must go to be with thy fathers, that I will raise up thy seed after thee, which shall be of thy sons; and I will establish his kingdom. He shall build me an house, and I will stablish his throne for ever. I will be his father, and he shall be my son: and I will not take my mercy away from him ... I will settle him in mine house and in my kingdom for ever: and his throne shall be established for evermore. ... David said, Who am I, O

Lord God . . . that thou hast brought me hitherto? And yet this was a small thing in thine eyes, O God; for thou hast also spoken of thy servant's house for a great while to come . . ."

David knew that God was only partially speaking of Solomon. He was also speaking of Jesus. In Luke the word of the Lord gives light on the mission of Jesus. *"The Lord shall give unto him the throne of his father David."*

Study the life of David and let it be prophetic for your life. See yourself running through a troop. See yourself leaping over a wall. See yourself breaking steel with your hands as David did in his ministry.

"I will give you the sure mercies of David."

Mercies can also be translated blessings or holy things. God gives to Jesus the blessings given to David. These blessings are also given to all believers since the believer is a joint heir with Jesus.

Open your understanding and receive the blessings of David rather than the garbage your situation in life hands out. Make your life produce the victories and blessings that belong to David's throne.

You are a king on a throne with Jesus. Call things into existence. A king commands and speaks and his servants obey. You are in Jesus. He is the king. Submit to Him, and He speaks and commands by placing thoughts and words into your mind and mouth.

"I will return and will build again the tabernacle of David."

This tabernacle is not an earthly tabernacle. It is the work of Jesus in the church. "The residue of men will seek the Lord, and all Gentiles..." This is a Gentile movement. Immediately before the return of Jesus, the Lord will probably deal directly with Israel, but right now we have everything that Israel rejected.

Jesus is building that tabernacle today through you and me.

EVERY BELIEVER HAS MORE THAN THE STRENGTH OF DAVID'S THRONE

Jesus said the believer would do greater works than He did upon earth because He was going to the Father. (John 14:12)

Ephesians 1:19-22 speaks of a greater power working in Christians, even the new power created at the resurrection of Jesus Christ from the dead. This power is in the believer now. It needs to be worked out.

Philippians 2:12 "... Work out your own salvation with fear and trembling."

The following verse says, *"For it is God which worketh in you both to will and to do of his good pleasure."* God has no limitations.

"With God nothing shall be impossible." Moving in God the believer has no limitations. Matthew 17:20: *"If you have faith . . . nothing shall be impossible with you."*

Zechariah 12:8 "In that day shall the Lord defend the inhabitants of Jerusalem; and he that is feeble among them at that day shall be as David; and the house of David shall be as God, as the angel of the Lord before them."

David slew a lion and a bear.

He slew a giant.

He did many exploits. All of his enemies submitted to him during his reign.

Get up and exercise your kingly authority.

The weak will be as David in our day.

We are to be as God unto the people about us.

Look at Peter in Acts 3. He told the man to get up and walk, and the man was healed.

Look at him in Acts 9:34. He told Aeneas to get up and be healed. He was.

Paul did the same in Acts 14:10. *"He said with a loud voice, stand upright on thy feet. And he leaped and walked."*

They did not pray. They released Jesus. They were as God unto the needy people of their day.

God will not share His glory with your flesh. The flesh cannot get into the act. You must be submitted to the spirit. This has to be an act of Jesus' faith flowing through you.

I heard of a lady who was led by the Spirit of God to visit a rest home. An old man was crying out for help. She went into his room and ministered to him. He put his hand to her cheek and said, "Thank you, Jesus. Thank you, Jesus." She was as Jesus to that man. He died three hours later.

I have seen similar things happen in our ministry. As we ministered people accepted it as if it were Jesus.

CHAPTER 2

DAVID'S THRONE IS SYMBOLIC OF LIFE IN CHRIST

In the previous chapter we saw that David's throne was prophetic of the believer. Prophetically Jesus was to sit on David's throne. Jesus fulfilled that prophecy.

Each believer is a joint heir with Jesus. Jesus is a king. The believer is a king. He is also a priest because Jesus is a priest. The believer has Jesus' glory. (John 17:22) The believer has His strength. Ephesians 6:10: *"Be strong in the Lord and in the power of His might."* The full resurrection power is at the believer's disposal. Nothing shall be impossible for the believer who operates in Jesus' faith.

See yourself a king.
See yourself a miracle worker.
Think like a king.
Do not submit to daily problems and difficulties. See your kingly ministry working things out for you and those about you. Peo-

ple are being ministered to in a very positive and helpful way through your life. Think of yourself as a blessing to your own life. See yourself setting people free when they come to you for help. See yourself changing the world about you.

ANOINTED MEN ON DAVID'S THRONE

1 Chronicles 11:6 "David said, Whosoever smitteth the Jebusites first shall be chief and captain. So Joab ... went first up, and was chief."

1 Chronicles 11:10 "These also are the chief of the mighty men whom David had, who strengthened themselves with him in his kingdom, and with all Israel, to make him king ..."

1 Chronicles 11:17-18 "David longed, and said, Oh that one would give me drink of the water of the well of Bethlehem, that is at the gate! And the three brake through the host of the Philistines, and drew water out of the well of Bethlehem, that was by the gate, and took it, and brought it to David: but David would not drink of it, but poured it out to the Lord."

David was a powerful man. He slew the lion and the bear by the power of God. He killed the giant by the power of the Lord. He shared this anointing with his men. They drew from his spirit.

Joab arose and went up after the enemy and became David's captain for most of his reign. Be daring in your thoughts and actions. Take your place as the leader in your kingdom. God will honor this just as he honored Joab under David's throne.

David longed for water from home. Three men fearlessly brought that water to him by breaking through enemy lines. Leadership is not for lazy and fearful men.

Fear caused one man to hide his talent. Jesus considered this man a failure.

David's men were fearless. They were completely submitted. You are to be submitted to Jesus. You are to be fearless. Step out and do what no other person has ever accomplished.

People today are crossing through enemy territory. Some are carrying Bibles. Some are stepping out in faith and forcing demons to retreat. Some are housewives standing in the gap for their family. Great soldiers are being born every day.

I knew a girl in Europe who carried Bibles into forbidden lands for several years. She was only 18 when she began.

The anointing of your King David, Jesus, is still passing down to His men today.

1 Chronicles 11:20 "Abishai the brother of Joab, he was chief of the three: for lifting up his spear against three hundred,

he slew them, and had a name among the three."

This man had so much of the spirit of David on him that he took on three hundred men and killed every one of them.

1 John 2:27 speaks of Jesus' anointing being upon you. Drink it into your life. See yourself operating in the anointing of Jesus. Confess that Jesus' anointing is working in you. You, too, are doing great exploits.

Great business miracles flow from Jesus through you. Great stories could be told here of business exploits accomplished through Jesus' power and anointing. Millions have been made in single transactions.

One man told me he was trying to get out of business. He would offer ridiculously low prices for antiques and people would sell them to him regardless. He was sincere and did not want to buy, but folks would just dump things on him at these low, low prices. I told him this was probably God's way of keeping him in this business.

I know a junk dealer who bought some junk batteries for $40.00 and sold them for $40,000. All of this money went to the mission field.

These are only small testimonies. Many of you could tell of great miracles in this area. Many more lie ahead for you and others. See it happening in your life.

1 Chronicles 11:22-23 "Benaiah the son of Jehoiada . . . he slew two lion-like men of Moab: also he went down and slew a lion in a pit in a snowy day. And he slew an Egyptian, a man of great stature, five cubits high; and in the Egyptian's hand was a spear like a weaver's beam; and he went down to him with a staff, and plucked the spear out of the Egyptian's hand, and slew him with his own spear."

You do not wait for better weather to do the job that faces you. You do not make excuses. You do it when the opportunity opens for you to act.

He went right down into the pit with the lion and slew him on a snowy day. He did not have the best equipment. He took what he had in his hand. It was only a stick.

This reminds one of the boy's lunch in the hands of Jesus. It got the job done.

This man, Benaiah, did not have the latest degree. He went down with the power of God, took the enemy's spear away from him, and killed him with his own weapon.

You do not have to wait for things to line up in your favor. You have God and that makes you stronger than the enemy. Stop making excuses.

David was a great man. He shared this strength with those who loved him and worked with him. Jesus does this for you.

Ephesians 4:11-15 "He gave some apostles ... prophets ... evangelists ... pastors and teachers. For the perfecting of the saints, for the work of the ministry, for the edifying of the body of Christ. Till we all come in the unity of the faith, and of the knowledge of the Son of God, unto a perfect man, unto the measure of the stature of the fulness of Christ ... speaking the truth in love, may grow up into him in all things, which is the head, even Christ:"

This speaks of God giving gifts to men. These men in turn share their lives and gifts with the entire church. The entire church then is brought to the maturity of Jesus. Each person is brought to the measure of the stature of the fulness of Christ. Each believer then is to grow up into Jesus in all things.

Jesus set the example. The scriptures say you are to imitate Jesus. (Ephesians 5:1) You are to follow His steps. (1 Peter 2:21) You have power to tread on serpents. (Luke 10:19) You can do all things through Jesus Christ. (Philippians 4:13) Your David, Jesus Christ, shares His victories with you. You are on His team.

MANY REVELATIONS ON DAVID'S THRONE

2 Chronicles 9:2 "And Solomon told her all her questions: and there was nothing

hid from Solomon..."

David operated in revelation knowledge continually. If you have any doubt about this, look at the many psalms that David received from the Lord.

Solomon picked up this same anointing from the Lord and through David, his father. Solomon wrote many proverbs and also received by divine revelation many truths which have been lost to us today. (1 Kings 4:32-33 and 2 Chronicles 9:29)

Jesus, the real David, certainly operated in revelation knowledge and taught his followers to do so.

Paul operated in supernatural gifts of the spirit.

The early church was so powerful because of the supernatural revelation knowledge operating in the lives of the believers that it soon covered the known world with the gospel of Jesus Christ.

You too must open yourself to the supernatural revelation gifts and let them minister to your generation.

Confess the following scriptures often.

John 1:50 "...Thou shalt see greater things than these."

1 Corinthians 14:1 "Follow after charity, and desire spiritual gifts, but rather that ye may prophesy."

1 Corinthians 14:39 "Covet to prophesy..."

1 Corinthians 12:31 "Covet earnestly the best gifts..."

Go over these scriptures. Make them personal. I shall see greater things. I will follow after love. I do desire spiritual gifts. I will prophesy. I will covet to prophesy.

Step out and begin to operate in the gifts. Do this gently but firmly. You may make mistakes. As you continue to try, you will sooner or later hit the flow and learn to work with the spirit. It is like anything else; you learn by doing.

GREAT FAVOR ON DAVID'S THRONE

Zechariah 12:10 "I will pour upon the house of David ... the spirit of grace (favor) and of supplications..."

This was directly fulfilled in Jesus' life.

Luke 2:40: "... The grace of God was upon him."

Luke 2:52: "Jesus increased in wisdom and stature, and in favour with God and man."

Grace is favor that you do not merit.

God poured out favor on David's throne. He did not deserve mercy. He failed God terriby on different occasions. This is exemplified when he took Bathsheba and murdered her husband. God forgave him and favored him.

Get our book *Favor, the Road to Success* and read it over about fifty times. Get this ministry of favor working in your life.

Many have been greatly blessed by operating in this favor of our Jesus David.

Families have been united.

Jobs have opened up.

Bad situations have been corrected.

Confessing God's laws of favor will change your life too.

Confess that He is pouring favor into your life today.

See yourself as a king on a throne higher than David's.

See yourself operating in favor in all situations during the day.

A banker told me that he had the law of favor operating in his bank. He goes to work excited. He expects favor to operate with his customers and also with his staff.

God's favor is poured out on you, King David.

Often I have seen people stand in line to give me a testimony about God's favor in their lives. Many miracles have come to God's children through operating in this law of favor.

WISDOM ON DAVID'S THRONE

2 Chronicles 1:12 "Wisdom and knowledge is granted unto thee; and I will give thee riches, and wealth, and

honor . . ."

This was spoken to Solomon, David's son, who was also part of David's throne. All of David's descendants who sat on his throne inherited these blessings in part. The full blessing is for you.

Solomon had more wisdom than any other king when he operated in God's blessings. Later he destroyed a large part of his wisdom because he worshipped other gods.

You have inherited the wisdom of Jesus Christ.

1 Corinthians 1:30 "But of him are ye in Christ Jesus, who of God is made unto us wisdom."

Ephesians 1:8 "Wherein he hath abounded toward us in all wisdom and prudence."

David's wisdom and Solomon's wisdom were only a type and shadow of your wisdom through Jesus Christ.

The scripture in Ephesians 1:8 says that he has abounded toward us all wisdom and prudence. The Greek could be interpreted: "He hath overflowed to you wisdom and intelligence."

You have an overflow of wisdom.
Confess it.
Believe it.
Use it.
Live in it.

Be the king you really are in Jesus. Live like a king in thought and action. Get your kingly ministry operating.

MUCH WEALTH ON DAVID'S THRONE

2 Samuel 12:30 "He took their king's crown from off his head, the weight whereof was a talent of gold with the precious stones: and it was set on David's head. And he brought forth the spoil of the city in great abundance."

2 Chronicles 9:13 "Now the weight of gold that came to Solomon in one year was six hundred and three score and six talents of gold."

2 Chronicles 9:27 "And the king made silver in Jerusalem as stones..."

It was previously quoted from 2 Chronicles 1:12: *"I will give thee riches, wealth, and honor."*

Solomon became the richest king of his day. Jesus said, *"Seek ye first the kingdom of God, and his righteousness; and all these things shall be added unto you."* (Matthew 6:33) Things here refers to houses, lands, and other material things.

The Lord does not want you to love money. He wants you to have riches to do the work you are called to do in this life.

2 Corinthians 8:9 tells you that Jesus became poor that you might be rich.

See yourself prosperous financially. A king usually has some money. You expect your kingdom to produce some money for you to carry on in that kingdom.

Many people think it is a sin to prosper, and those thoughts prevent them from walking in prosperity. Many good Christians fail at this point. Ignorance of your inheritance will cause you to walk in poverty.

Keep your heart on Jesus. Love Him. Seek Him. The money you need to do His work will flow in super abundance.

ALL ENEMIES DESTROYED ON DAVID'S THRONE

David had rest round about him after everything was accomplished. He had many battles during his lifetime, but he turned a peaceful kingdom over to Solomon.

Jesus defeated the enemy for you. He won all the battles for you. Colossians 2:15: *"Having spoiled principalities and powers . . ."*

The enemy may try to raise his head, but he is defeated. Look at the enemy through the cross. Stop fearing a defeated enemy.

You are to possess the gate of your enemy. Go to it. Bring in the finances into God's kingdom. Bring in the best businesses. Bring in the best farms and ranches. Bring in the best jobs. Rise up, ye kings of Jesus, and manifest your victories.

2 Samuel 7:9 "I was with thee whither-

soever thou wentest, and have cut off all thine enemies out of thy sight, and have made thee a great name, like unto the name of the great men that are in the earth."

1 Chronicles 17:8 & 10 "I have been with thee whithersoever thou hast walked, and have cut off all thine enemies from before thee, and have made thee a name like the name of the great men that are in the earth ... moreover I will subdue all thine enemies..."

Every enemy that stood against David fell. This is what Jesus has done for you likewise. He has given you *"Power to tread on serpents and scorpions, and over all the power of the enemy: and nothing shall by any means hurt you."* (Luke 10:19) Yes, He has "spoiled principalities and powers..."

Solomon inherited David's victories. None dared raise up against Solomon until he began to worship pagan gods. Little by little he gave demonic forces a place in his life. It was then that the enemy began to lift its head against his kingdom.

The church inherited Jesus' victory. She was indestructible. Then sin began to creep into the churches. Sin robbed the church and the believers of the power of the throne.

Set your face to serve the Lord by complete dedication and positive faith. You too will return to the full benefits of the kingdom handed over to you at the resurrection of Jesus Christ.

Confess your kingly throne.
Think on it.
Let this throne life come alive in you.
No enemy can stand against you.
Smile and step out today and conquer.

GREAT MULTITUDES ON DAVID'S THRONE

1 Chronicles 12:22 "For at that time day by day there came to David to help him, until it was a great host, like the host of God."

David was anointed of God to lead Israel. Men were drawn to him and they became a great and powerful army. It truly was "like the host of God."

This same spirit manifested itself in Jesus' ministry. Everywhere Jesus went multitudes were gathered to him. One scripture said, "He could not be hid." He was always in demand. Five thousand men plus women and children followed him as he tried to escape into the mountains for a rest. At every turn in His ministry the multitudes were gathered together.

At one time Jesus was in a home so crowded that no one could get to him. Some men brought a sick man to be healed. His friends had to take him to the roof and let him down to Jesus on ropes.

The disciples and early church inherited this anointing. Three thousand were saved on the day of Pentecost. A few days later there were five thousand believers in Jesus. (Acts 4:4) In Acts 21:20 thousands of Jews believed. About two hundred and fifty years later, under Constantine, the church had gained so much influence that it was recognized as the state religion. This became her downfall as things became too easy for the believer. Believers gradually yielded to ease and luxury until their kingdom was practically taken from them.

Now, after years of struggle, the church has been regaining her kingdom. Jesus handed it down to the church full of power and victory. Sin robbed the church. Now she is fighting back through the "fog and the smog" and is regaining her rightful place.

The full kingly ministry is being restored.

Miracle faith is raising to new levels daily.

Excitement is everywhere.

MUCH FAME ON DAVID'S THRONE

1 Chronicles 14:17 "The fame of David went out into all lands; and the Lord brought the fear of him upon all nations."

Luke 4:14 " . . . There went out a fame of him (Jesus) through all the region

round about."

David was a very famous king. All the lands feared and trembled at the mention of his name. They were all subject to him and paid taxes to David.

Jesus, your king, had the same spirit. He inherited this from the Father. "There went out a fame of him through all the region round about."

Jesus Christ in you is still famous. Your ministry is famous. Your position on the job is famous. Your life is famous.

You (because of Jesus in you) are famous. Your church (because of Christ in the church) is famous.

Confess this fame. Believe this law. Let it come alive. You are not a king on a defeated, unwanted, and unknown throne. You are a king on a very famous throne. Let this fame come alive. Confess this over and over.

People will begin to speak of your ministry, and they will come to you as they did to King Jesus when he walked this earth.

They will speak of your church and will cause many to come and worship the Lord with you.

People will be drawn to your business.

People will want you around.

Always remember to smile as you reign on this wonderful throne.

Repossess your land of fame. Satan has taken God's people downhill too long. It may take you a little while to recapture this, but you can do it. Remember to draw near to the Lord. Most of you will see miracles now and then in this area.

If you are a pastor, get your people to thinking of multitudes rather than handfuls.

Get your company to confessing larger sales, etc.

I have seen our ministry begin to change as we constantly confess that Jesus Christ in us is still famous. He still draws the multitudes.

MUCH JOY ON DAVID'S THRONE

2 Samuel 6:16 "And as the ark of the Lord came into the city of David, Michal Saul's daughter looked through a window and saw king David leaping and dancing before the Lord; and she despised him in her heart."

2 Chronicles 9:7 "Happy are thy men, and happy are these thy servants, which stand continually before thee, and hear thy wisdom."

David knew how to release joy. He knew how to "get happy" before the Lord. He leaped and he danced before the Lord. Solomon's throne, which was a continuation of David's throne inherited this joy. The Queen of Sheba reported of this throne that, "Happy are thy men, and happy are thy servants."

Hebrews 1:9 "...God ... hath anointed thee with the oil of gladness above thy fellows."

This Greek word translated gladness means leaping joy. In Acts 16:35 the jailor was very much filled with joy. He had just been baptized. He "Set meat before them, and rejoiced..." This word "rejoiced" is the same as the one for "gladness" in Hebrews 1:9. The Amplified Bible translates this as follows: "He set food before them; and he leaped much for joy and exulted..."

Your kingdom is a kingdom of joy. Jesus had a joy that was expressive as well as the calm, peaceful joy demonstrated in other passages.

The early church had this joy. They inherited it from Jesus. In Acts 8:8: *"There was great joy in the city."* In 2 Corinthians 7:4: *"...I am exceeding joyful in all our tribulations."* Galatians 5:22: *"The fruit of the spirit is love, joy..."* 1 Thessalonians 1:6: *"...In much affliction, with joy of the Holy Ghost."*

David had much joy, but the spirit of Saul was in his wife, Michal. She hated the real freedom and joy of the Holy Ghost. This hatred caused her womb to be closed. She bore no children because of this.

Jesus had this joy. Paul had joy in the midst of persecution. The fruit of the spirit is joy.

The fruit of religion is a long face.

True joy and real worship are again being manifested in the kingdom.

GREAT DELIVERANCES ON DAVID'S THRONE

1 Chronicles 14:11 "... David smote them there. Then David said, God hath broken in upon mine enemies ... like the breaking forth of waters: ..."

When a dam breaks, the water sweeps down through the valleys below destroying everything in its path. God did this for David. He was like a mighty rushing river destroying anything that stood in his path.

Jesus met every devil with this same force. No force could stand in his presence. Many demons screamed and begged for mercy when they came face to face with Jesus Christ the Son of God. They all left at His command.

This same power is transmitted to you as you share Jesus' throne.

Mark 16:17 "... In my name shall they cast out devils ..."

Acts 5:15 "... They brought forth the sick into the streets and laid them on beds and couches, that at the least the shadow of Peter passing by might overshadow some of them."

Acts 5:16 "There came also a multitude out of the cities round

about unto Jerusalem, bringing sick folks, and them which were vexed with unclean spirits: and they were healed every one."

Acts 10:38 "God anointed Jesus of Nazareth with the Holy Ghost and with power: who went about doing good, and healing all that were oppressed of the devil; for God was with him."

Acts 8:5-7 "Then Philip went down to the city of Samaria, and preached Christ unto them. And the people with one accord gave heed unto those things which Philip spake, hearing, and seeing the miracles which he did. For unclean spirits, crying with loud voices, came out of many that were possessed with them..."

Acts 14:10 "(Paul) said with a loud voice, Stand upright on thy feet. And he leaped and walked."

Yes, the church has inherited the throne of David. Whether it was Jesus walking on earth during his ministry or Jesus walking in Peter, Philip, Paul, or some other believer, there was great deliverance like the breaking forth of many waters. Every power that stood in their path to resist them was destroyed. Healings took place. Demons were cast out. Joy entered in place of gloom and sadness.

Great deliverances are being manifested in the kingdom again. The great Pentecostal revivals during the first half of this century broke out like the "breaking forth of many waters." People from all walks of life were healed, delivered, and set free. Financial blessings accompanied many of these deliverances.

Once again a great revival of deliverance is flowing from David's throne. Many are being set free. The Word is breaking forth like the "Breaking out of many waters." Financial victories are being seen. Healing of the bodies is present. Emotions are being healed. David's throne is still effective in this world today.

See yourself moving in this deliverance. See demons submitting to your ministry in Jesus' name. See the sick being healed through your faith. See yourself being used in miracles. This is your throne. Do not let another take your place. This is your hour to demonstrate the power of Jesus Christ in the land. Refuse to sit back in the shadows. Come forth, thou King.

GREAT MIRACLES ON DAVID'S THRONE

1 Chronicles 11:5 "And the inhabitants of Jebus said to David, Thou shalt not come hither. Nevertheless David took the castle of Zion . . ."

The inhabitants of Jebus said, "Thou shalt

not come in hither." David must have thought they had said, "Come in." He charged forward and took the castle and dwelt therein himself.

Jesus healed the blind. He opened deaf ears. He healed all types of sickness. He was a miracle worker.

You have inherited this ministry. You must go heal. You must go and release miracles.

Jesus told the seventy to go heal the sick in Luke 10:9. They were to announce that the kingdom of God was in them. *"Heal the sick that are therein, and say unto them, The kingdom of God is come nigh unto you."* Luke 17:21 says, *"The kingdom of God is within you."*

You are God's relay station. *"Out of your heart are the issues (sources) of life."* (Proverbs 4:23)

You are to release love.

You are to release the gifts.

You are to release healings.

Peter said, *"Such as I have, give I thee."* (Acts 3:6)

Drill this into your spirit. Let these words sink into your mind. You are a joint-heir with Jesus. You are his co-worker. 2 Corinthians 6:1: *"We . . . as workers together with him."*

Jesus is the vine and you are the branch. (John 15:5) The life of Jesus is flowing right out through you, the branch.

You are supposed to produce. It is normal

for the branch to operate in cooperation with the vine. *"All things are yours."* (1 Corinthians 3:21) You do not need anything. You are already complete in Christ. You are a king.

Act like it.

Think like it.

Produce like it.

Matthew 11:29 speaks of being yoked up with Jesus. His burden is light. You share His yoke and you are sharing His throne.

Be a faithful king. Go and expect miracles. Confess miracles. Expect miracles to be normal for your life. Anything less is under par for you.

THE FLESH MAY TRY TO GIVE YOU TROUBLE ON DAVID'S THRONE

2 Samuel 3:1 "Now there was long war between the house of Saul and the house of David: but David waxed stronger and stronger, and the house of Saul waxed weaker and weaker."

Because of Saul's sin, after his death, the kingdom was given to David. But some of Saul's house did not want to accept the inevitable. The two houses warred against each other. The house of David was victorious.

Galatians 5:17 "The flesh lusteth against the Spirit, and the Spirit against the flesh: and these are contrary the one to the other; so that ye cannot do the things

that ye would."

Galatians 4:29 "As then he that was born after the flesh persecuted him that was born after the Spirit, even so it is now."

Galatians 5:24 "They that are Christ's have crucified the flesh with the affections and lusts."

The flesh must be held down. The flesh wars against the spirit. These are contrary. Paul speaks of keeping *"under his body."* (1 Corinthians 9:27)

Galatians 4:22-31 compares Hagar's children to the children of the flesh. Isaac, the child of Sarah is symbolic of the spiritual line. The children of Ishmael, (Hagar's son) persecuted the children of Isaac (Sarah's son). Thus you have, "He that was born after the flesh persecuted him that was born after the Spirit, even so it is now."

The flesh still tries to arise and bring you into bondage. As you move on to know the Lord, you will "crucify the flesh." The flesh must not control the king on David's throne.

As you submit to Jesus, the flesh is put down and the spirit gains strength. Real kingdom life begins when the flesh is down and the Spirit is Lord.

MANY VICTORIES MAY CAUSE YOU TO BECOME SOFT ON DAVID'S THRONE

2 Samuel 5:12-13 "And David perceived

that the Lord had established him king over Israel, and that he had exalted his kingdom for his people Israel's sake. David took him more concubines and wives out of Jerusalem."

David was blessed of God. He was established as king over Israel. His next move was to turn to the flesh. He took more concubines and wives.

Later David took another man's wife, committed adultery with her, and finally murdered her husband.

The history of Israel shows that they followed the same route. God would bless them and then they would turn to the arm of flesh. Adultery, fornication, lusts of all types, idol worship, and the love of luxury constantly rose to destroy the work of God. Jesus likened this to thorns or the care of this world and the deceitfulness of riches which choke the word and make it unfruitful.

The history of denominationalism is the same. They start out fairly hungry for truth, but when they are established they slowly begin to be loyal to man's ideas rather than the Word of God.

DELIVERANCE FROM REBELLION ON DAVID'S THRONE

1 Samuel 28:17-18 "And the Lord hath done to him, as he spake by me: for the Lord hath rent the kingdom out of thine

hand, and given it to thy neighbour, even to David: Because thou obeyedst not the voice of the Lord..."

Saul refused to obey the Lord. Saul was rejected as king. David was given the kingdom.

Judas rebelled against the Lord and lost his life, ministry, and salvation, if he ever had salvation.

Paul and others took his place.

Men may rise up against you in your business, on the job, in the church, or in the neighborhood. Stay clean. Stay steady. Confess favor. Love everyone involved. Bless your enemies. Keep moving in the Spirit of the Lord. You, too, will soon be established king in that situation in which rebellious Sauls have tried to hinder you.

Your authority may be challenged or undermined, but it cannot long be challenged if you apply the principles of the kingdom. These principles are positive faith, honesty, love, compassion, and wisdom.

Leaders in the body of Christ who fall into error will sooner or later be removed or sidelined from the main flow opening the way for others to take their places. The real kingdom of the Lord will continue to march forward.

YOU RECOVER ALL ON DAVID'S THRONE

1 Samuel 30:18-19 "And David recovered all that the Amalekites had carried away

... there was nothing lacking to them, neither small or great ... David recovered all."

David returned home that day with his men. The Amalekites had taken his property, his wives, and his children. They had burned David's town. David went after them, overcame them, and recovered all.

Think on this.

Visualize it happening in your life.

Visualize your finances multiplying.

Visualize your family flowing in harmony.

Visualize the recovering of the full ministry of Jesus. This is what redemption is all about. You are purchased from the kingdom of Satan. You are translated into the kingdom of God through Jesus Christ our Lord. You have been purchased by the blood of Jesus Christ. You belong in the kingdom of Jesus. You owe it to the Lord to live like kings in His kingdom. You are no longer under the Adamic nature. You are of the second man, the Lord of heaven.

STOP FLEEING FROM THE ENEMY

1 Chronicles 11:14 "They set themselves in the midst of that parcel, and delivered it, and slew the Philistines; and the Lord saved them by a great deliverance."

You may have to run for a period of time until you can organize yourself, but the time must come when you set yourself in Jesus' name and deliver yourself.

Operate all of these areas by faith.

Form a picture in your mind of your victory.

See yourself blessed.

See yourself at peace enjoying the full blessings of the Lord.

MEN OF TALENT ON DAVID'S THRONE

1 Chronicles 12:2 "They were armed with bows, and could use both the right hand and the left in hurling stones and shooting arrows..."

The spirit of God gives gifts to men. He is raising up men with many talents to sit on the throne with king David Jesus.

The body of Christ is filled with people who are full of many talents. They are capable of doing many exploits.

Churches should confess these men and women into their fellowships to fill the needs in that local body. They should also confess these people into their ministry beyond that local body. In this day we need capable men and women to come forth with many new ideas to meet the needs of our day. There are many ministries besides preaching and teaching the word that desperately need to come forth.

A SPIRIT LED SUBMISSION TO LEADERSHIP ON DAVID'S THRONE

1 Chronicles 12:17-18 "David went out to meet them, and answered and said unto them, If ye be come peaceably unto me to help me, mine heart shall be knit unto you: but if ye be come to betray me to mine enemies, seeing there is no wrong in mine hands, the God of our fathers look thereon, and rebuke it. Then the spirit came upon Amasai, who was chief of the captains, and he said, Thine are we, David, and on thy side ... then David received them, and made them captains of the band."

These men came to help David. They came to flow with him. They did not come to dictate policy or rebel against his program.

There are still Judases in the camp who wait for their opportunity to stab the pastor in the back. May these people be thinned out of the ranks as soon as possible. There must be spirit-led submission to God's leaders. This is not a blind submission. David's heart was right toward them. Jesus is our David. His heart surely is right toward us.

Pastors are undershepherds. You will submit to them on a spirit-led basis, but it will not be bondage. It will be what God joins. Any moment that you cannot flow with your leaders, then you need to truly seek the Lord.

If you are at fault, make an adjustment. After seeking God and good counsel, if you honestly feel that you cannot flow with the leadership, make some changes. God has a place for you. Do not divide the body with carnal approaches.

Many people are very immature and try to control the church. In some cases men are really leaders and need to find their place of leadership in something else. But do not try to take the pastor's leadership from him.

The pastor is not to be a dictator. There are some things he needs to share with the congregation and work things out together with them.

1 Chronicles 13:1-4 "David consulted with the captains of thousands and hundreds, and with every leader. And David said unto all the congregation of Israel. If it seem good unto you, and that it be of the Lord our God, let us send abroad unto our brethren every where, that are left in all the land of Israel, and with them also to the priests and Levites which are in their cities and suburbs, that they may gather themselves unto us: And let us bring again the ark of our God to us ... and all the congregation said that they would do so: for the thing was right in the eyes of all the people."

Jesus, our David, did only what the Father

told him to do. Undershepherds must be spirit led. There will be times when he will consult the people on decisions and there will be times when he will be directed to make decisions dictated to him alone by the Holy Ghost.

NEW CART THEOLOGY IS STILL PLAGUING DAVID'S THRONE

1 Chronicles 13:7-11 "They carried the ark of God in a new cart out of the house of Abinadab: and Uzza and Ahio drave the cart. And David and all Israel played before God with all their might, and with singing, and with harps... when they came unto the threshing floor of Chidon, Uzza put forth his hand to hold the ark; for the oxen stumbled. And the anger of the Lord was kindled against Uzza, and he smote him, because he put his hand to the ark: and there he died before God. And David was displeased because the Lord had made a preach upon Uzza..."

God's plan was for the ark to be carried on poles by the priests. David with his new cart theology went against God's word. It got him in trouble. Uzza was killed for touching the ark. This was specifically forbidden by God. Only the priests and Levites were allowed to touch the ark.

There are many new cart programs on David's throne today. Men are still rebelling against God's program, and they will have the same problems. God will not bless flesh programs. Flesh programs will still destroy and bring hurt to the body of Christ.

May we seek out God's program and follow it.

ENEMIES TO DAVID'S THRONE

1 Chronicles 14:9 "The Philistines came and spread themselves in the valley of Rephaim."

Satan will have his Philistines camped against David's throne today. You will find them there quite often. Upon reading the following verses you will find that David inquired of God about how to destroy the enemy. God gave them the victory. David's own report of the battle was: "God hath broken in upon mine enemies by mine hand like the breaking forth of waters."

When the church seeks the Lord, God will always give them the right strategy to overcome the enemy.

GOD HAS MADE A COVENANT WITH DAVID

Psalm 89:3-4 "I have made a covenant with my chosen, I have sworn unto David my servant, Thy seed will I establish for ever, and build up thy throne to all generations."

This covenant is in operation today in the

church. The blessings of David are fully manifested in Jesus and His seed. We are the true seed of David through Jesus Christ. Jesus is building His throne in the earth today. It will never be defeated. The church is on the march and knows no defeat.

If you will recall, many of David's direct descendants were recipients of the blessings of this covenant. Judah would be in sin. The king who was often largely responsible for this sin was one of David's family. The prophet would tell him that the kingdom would have to be judged because of their sin. Then a covenant blessing would come. The prophet would tell the king that the full judgment would not come as long as he lived for David His servant's sake. This covenant with David operated in all of his descendants. Our covenant is much more powerful today. This is why the mercy of God is so strongly manifested in the body of Christ today. Men can do some terrible things and God still blesses His under-Davids.

Do not use this as an excuse to sin. Remember David's sin with Bathsheba cost him in many ways. The child died and the kingdom suffered.

2 Samuel 12:9-15 "Wherefore hast thou despised the commandment of the Lord, to do evil in his sight? Thou hast killed Uriah the Hittite with the sword, and hast taken his wife to be thy wife, and

hast slain him with the sword of the children of Ammon. Now therefore the sword shall never depart from thine house ... I will rise up evil against thee out of thine own house, and I will take thy wives before thine eyes, and give them unto thy neighbour, and he shall lie with thy wives in the sight of this sun ... David said ... I have sinned against the Lord. And Nathan said unto David, The Lord also hath put away thy sin; thou shalt not die ... the child also that is born unto thee shall surely die ... and the Lord struck the child that Uriah's wife bare unto David, and it was very sick."

Do not throw Old Testament teachings to one side. They are given for you for examples. *"Now these things were our examples, to the intent we should not lust after evil things, as they also lusted."* (1 Corinthians 10:6) *"For whatsoever things were written aforetime were written for our learning..."* (Romans 15:4)

You will find many rich and interesting things when you follow the Davidic covenant throughout the scriptures. Keep your eyes open. You may want to study all of Psalm 89. You will find some basic principles for the church in this psalm.

CHAPTER 3

REIGNING FROM THE THRONE

YOU REIGN BY JESUS CHRIST

Romans 5:17 "... Shall reign in life by one, Jesus Christ."

Romans 8:37 "Nay, in all these things we are more than conquerors through him that loved us."

Isaiah 40:10 "The Lord will come with strong hand, and his arm shall rule for him: behold, his reward is with him, and his work before him."

Matthew 2:6 "... Shall come a Governor, that shall rule my people Israel."

2 Timothy 2:12 "If we suffer, we shall also reign with him..."

"Shall reign in life by one, Jesus Christ."

You are to reign or rule in this life over situations by Jesus Christ. This same word *reign* is used in Revelation 19:6: "... *For the*

Lord God omnipotent reigneth." It is also used for believers reigning in Revelation 20:4: *"... They lived and reigned with Christ a thousand years."* Jesus Christ reigns through you today. Paul said, "Christ liveth in me." Jesus Christ is alive and well in you today. Let him reign over situations here and now.

"More than conquerors through Him."

This literally means conquering with power to spare. You are so powerful that you can go beyond the norm and do exploits that are not expected of man.

Christ at the right hand of God is all-powerful. He is in you by the Spirit. Do not limit Him with your earthly mind. Do not block Him with your earthly or carnal will.

"His arm shall rule for him."

Rule means to have or make to have dominion. It means a governor. It also means to have power.

Christ is the arm of God. He is the governor. He has dominion over every situation. Nothing on earth perturbed him. They could not crucify Him until He submitted to it. He declared openly that no one could take His life from Him. He laid it down of himself.

Jesus Christ in you is still the arm of God. The power that is invested in you is reigning or ruling power. You have no wants. You are complete in Jesus. Everything you will ever need is already yours in Jesus Christ. You are more than a conqueror. You are to rule through Jesus Christ over every situation.

Visualize the spirit of authority entering into every part of your being. See strength flowing into every cell and muscle of your spiritual and physical being. Never meditate on defeat, failure, or problems. Constantly come above the negative.

"Shall come a governor, that shall rule my people."

A governor is the head or ruler in any given area. Governors are usually under someone. This same Greek word was used in reference to Joseph being governor in Egypt. Jesus is under the Father.

The Jesus in you is governor under the Father. 1 Corinthians 15:28: *"When all things shall be subdued unto him, then shall the Son also himself be subject unto him that put all things under him, that God may be all in all."*

Jesus, the governor, is ruling His people through you. He speaks through you. He heals through you. He performs miracles through you. He is very much alive in this world today through your life.

If a governor had a need, he would give the command, and it would be met. Move into the spirit realm. All needs are met through Jesus Christ. Speak the words of authority. Give some commands and expect them to be carried out. You are in charge when you are in the flow of the spirit.

"If we suffer, we shall also reign with him..."

Endure patiently would be a good translation for the word here translated *suffer*. Stay behind, remain, undergo, bear trials, have fortitude, persevere, abide, take patiently, or tarry behind are also good synonyms for the original word translated *suffer*.

Hang in there, remain cool under all circumstances, be patient in trials. Be willing to be temporarily left behind at certain points. Your day will come.

Look beyond the immediate problem. See yourself reigning on the job regardless of present circumstances. Look beyond the circumstances. Visualize the throne principle of reigning and ruling operating on your behalf. See your governorship being activated. Know that things are working for you because you are drawing from a higher authority than eyes and circumstances can control. You are always in control even though it may not appear to be so at the time.

This Greek word translated suffer is used only once in the New Testament. The whole idea is to endure patiently. See yourself enduring patiently at all times.

YOU ARE TO RULE OVER YOUR OPPRESSOR

Esther 9:1 "... The Jews had rule over them that hated them."

Isaiah 14:2 "... They shall take them captives, whose captives they were; and they shall rule over their oppressors."

Both of these verses pertain to the Babylonian captivity. In Isaiah it is prophesied that they would be taken captive. Over and over this was spoken to Israel. God warned them to repent or the enemy would destroy their country and take them captive. It was during these times that God also told them that they would rule over their enemies. It was for this same period of Babylonian captivity that God told him (Israel) that they were to "Take them (the enemy) captives, whose captives they were; and they shall rule over their oppressors."

The Babylonian captivity finally came. Daniel soon became prime minister of Babylon and remained in this position for about 35 years during the reign of Nebuchadnezzar. Then later under Darius the Mede he again held a place of leadership in the country. It was at this time when Darius was planning to put Daniel over all the country that jealousy caused Daniel to be thrown into the lions' den.

Daniel ruled over his oppressors.

The three Hebrew children who were thrown into the fiery furnace were governors over different provinces. They came out of the fire without a smell of smoke and were promoted even further. These Hebrew children were part of those taken captive to Babylon from Jerusalem. They went from the bottom to the top.

The three Hebrew children ruled over their oppressors.

At the end of the captivity, after much of the remnant had returned to Jerusalem under the Persians, Esther, a Jew, was made queen. Mordecai was her uncle.

Mordecai was hated by Haman, the king's right hand man. Haman built a scaffold on which to hang Mordecai. He planned to kill all of the Jews. Esther exposed Haman to the king. Haman was then hanged on the scaffold he had built for Mordecai. Mordecai was then promoted to Haman's position as the king's right hand man. Many people in the land became Jews for the fear of Mordecai fell upon them. Thus Esther 9:1 is a fulfillment of Isaiah: "The Jews had rule over them that hated them."

Like all scriptures, this also applies to you today. At times you are to patiently endure as you believe. Your time will come. The breakthrough is for you. There is a season for each type of fruit or plant. Some have longer growing and maturing seasons. Watch your kingly ministry blossom and come into full strength. Anticipate the full ministry of the king coming forth in you.

YOU ARE TO RULE IN THE MIDST OF YOUR PROBLEM

Psalm 110:2 "The Lord shall send the rod of thy strength out of Zion: rule thou in the midst of thine enemies."

Jesus is the rod of thy strength.
Rule in the midst of your problem.
Do not wait for that perfect day.
Arise now and plow through to victory. Stop waiting for something special to come along. There is no perfect day. Press through. Jesus will meet you as you apply the principle of ruling in the midst of your pressure. Look at your pressure and laugh. You see beyond your problem. You know the natural does not have the last word. Your authority changes all present conditions into victory.

Be like Daniel whom we just mentioned. Although he was taken captive into Babylon as a defeated slave, he soon became next to the top ruler in the kingdom.

Right in the midst of your problem consider: *"He raiseth up the poor out of the dust, and lifteth up the beggar from the dunghill; to set them among princes."* (I Samuel 2:8)

You cannot "cry in your soup" any longer. God's program is to start where you are and recognize that the impossible one is in you.

The impossible life is yours.

You can do the impossible.

History is full of people who have had nothing one day and seemingly over night became very prosperous.

Recently I prophesied to a congregation of saints that someone there was sitting on a diamond mine, and prosperity would soon come to that person. A man in that congregation had just gone bankrupt. A couple of months later God began to prosper him. He knew this prophecy was for him. God blessed him in the midst of his problem. He ruled by Jesus Christ in the midst of trouble and came through victoriously.

"The Lord shall send the rod of thy strength . . . rule . . ."

Jesus has come.
Jesus is the rod of your strength.
You have His life.
You have His ability.
You have His strength.
You have His commission.
You have His anointing.
You have His life.

He set the example for you. Imitate His life. See His actions in the Word as an example for you to duplicate.

RULE BY WALKING IN WISDOM

Proverbs 8:11-18 "For wisdom is better

than rubies ... I wisdom dwell with prudence ... counsel is mine, and sound wisdom ... by me kings reign, and princes decree justice. By me princes rule, and nobles, even all the judges of the earth. I love them that love me; and those that seek me early shall find me. Riches and honour are with me; yea, durable riches and righteousness."

2 Samuel 23:3 "The God of Israel said ... He that ruleth over men must be just, ruling in the fear of God."

"Wisdom is better than rubies."

Wisdom produces rubies. Rubies cannot produce wisdom.

Jesus is your wisdom. (1 Corinthians 1:30)
His wisdom flows through you. His intelligence flows through you.

"Counsel is mine."

Counsel means opinion, deliberation or recommendation.

Walking in His wisdom means walking in the advice or counsel or guidance of Jesus Christ. This is yours. Claim it. See every move you make being directed by the Holy Ghost.

"By me kings reign."

It takes wisdom for a king to reign. Many of you kings need to see Jesus' advice flowing in all of your decisions.

You have Jesus' counsel.

You have Jesus' guidance.

It is there. See it working. You are reigning by Jesus Christ.

"Riches and honor are with me."

Prosperity comes to those who walk in the counsel and wisdom of God. Every born-again person has the ability to walk in Christ and demonstrate His wisdom. (There may be a few exceptions in mentally handicapped people.) With this wisdom comes success.

Occasionally people may seem to go backward. Usually there is a hang-up in their background or failure to use this wisdom. It is like trying to fill a bucket with water when it has holes in the bottom. The water will soon drain out.

I know of one man who received the fullness of the Spirit and continued to go backward for five years. Later he discovered his problem. He dealt with it and immediately began to reign as a king. He now has a good job and is very prosperous. Yes, you rule by walking in wisdom.

REIGN BY A STEADY SPIRIT

Colossians 3:15 "And let the peace of God rule in your hearts..."

Be calm and collected as best you can at all times. When the pressures hit, confess to yourself or a friend who would understand, "I let the peace of God rule in me right now.

His peace is taking over in this situation." Repeat this a few times. Feel this peace flooding every part of your being. Relax in it. Your emotions may or may not manifest this peace immediately. At the end of the day you will see that great things happened because you held a steady spirit. Practice this also when you are not under great stress and strain. Submit to His peace, and let it dominate your spirit and emotions.

REIGN OVER YOUR SPIRIT

Proverbs 25:28 "He that hath no rule over his own spirit is like a city that is broken down, and without walls."

Proverbs 16:32 "He that is slow to anger is better than the mighty; and he that ruleth his spirit than he that taketh a city."

See yourself calm and in full control of adverse situations. Work on this especially if you are a person with a short temper. Get quiet before the Lord and visualize yourself responding with love and kindness to all people, both kind and unkind. Rule over your spirit. These are kingdom laws, and the only way for you to succeed in this kingdom is to operate in its fundamental rules.

A person who is slow to anger is stronger and more effective than the mighty. He that ruleth his spirit is stronger than a conqueror who does great exploits.

If you do not control your spirit, the devil can overrun your life just as an enemy can overrun a country with no defenses. Maintain an attitude of tenderness, love, and forgiveness.

Stay steady, and the Lord will fight your battles.

Become angry, and all hell takes up its abode in you. You have breached your defenses. It is then that sickness can enter. It is then that problems grow and grow.

REIGN BY DETERMINATION

In the following scriptures from the Old Testament, diligence means determination.

The Greek word translated diligence in Romans 12:8 means speed, eagerness, earnestness, carefulness, diligence, forwardness, and haste.

Diligence according to Webster means to be steady and constant in application. It means industrious.

Romans 12:8 "... He that ruleth, with diligence..."

You reign by promptness. You do not put everything off till tomorrow.

You reign by being earnest, intent, or serious. You are steady. You are not fly-by-night in your operation.

You reign by being eager. You live excited. You are full of life.

You reign by carefulness. You make decisions with wisdom. You pray about situations. You seek counsel from wise people.

You are a steady person. You are consistent in operation. You can be trusted and relied upon to keep your word. You are industrious. You stay with it until the job is done. Then you get another goal and do the same with it until it is finished.

Proverbs 12:24 "The hand of the diligent shall bear rule: but the slothful shall be under tribute."

Proverbs 22:29 "Seest thou a man diligent in his business? He shall stand before kings; he shall not stand before mean men."

Proverbs 10:4 "He becometh poor that dealeth with a slack hand: but the hand of the diligent maketh rich."

Proverbs 21:5 "The thoughts of the diligent tend only to plenteousness; but every one that is hasty only to want."

Proverbs 13:4 "The soul of the sluggard desireth and hath nothing: but the soul of the diligent shall be made fat."

"The hand of the diligent shall bear rule."

If you are determined, you will rule eventually. Set your teeth and hang in there. Remember this word diligent in the Hebrew means determination.

Set your face like a flint.

You cannot be defeated. Close your eyes and see yourself walking in strength. See yourself walking right through every obstacle that stands between you and doing the perfect will of God.

"The slothful shall be under tribute."

Laziness gets you in trouble. Satan takes advantage of you. You do not get ahead by being lazy. It will put you in bondage to everyone.

"Seest thou a man diligent in his business? He shall stand before kings; he shall not stand before mean men."

Mean men are little men with no vision. You want to do business with strong men. You are to associate with kings. You are a king. You are to operate in the realm of success. God is success. Be determined that you shall reign in this life. Be determined that you shall stand with the most successful in this life. Do not see yourself walking with men of no vision. If little men continue to hold you back, change your position. Associate with strong men who love the Lord.

Glen Cunningham was burned when he was a child. He would never walk again, according to the doctor's report. The spirit of determination arose in Glen. He refused to believe the doctor's report. He moved above it. He became a champion runner and went on to win in the Olympics.

One lady was told she would soon die. Another lady was told she would soon recover from the same disease, tuberculosis. The lady with the light case had problems at home and had no fight in her. She soon died. The one who was told she would die was soon healed and out of the sanatorium. She had a good relationship at home and was determined to raise her family.

I met a lady a couple of years ago who was told by her doctor to go home and die. She had one scripture, "You shall live and not die." She said, "No, doctor, I shall go home and live." I saw her one year after the medical verdict. She was completely cured of cancer.

Red Grange had an accident as a boy while delivering ice. The doctors wanted to amputate his leg. He refused to have it done. He determined that he would not lose his leg. He went on in life and became a professional football player with the Greenbay Packers. He became a legend because of his prowess.

Phil Esposito could not walk until after his younger brother learned to walk. He was about three years old before he learned to walk. Both he and his brother played hockey later in life. However, Phil was so awkward he could not make the team in high school. His brother was chosen over him because of his agility.

As a child he would practice till he wore his brother down and then he would get his mother out to practice with him. He would practice with anyone he could get on the ice. He was determined. He is now in professional hockey. He still looks awkward, but he is also high scoreman.

"He becometh poor that dealeth with a slack hand: but the hand of the diligent maketh rich."

Slothfulness will steal your success and your kingship ministry. If you are determined, you will be rich (successful). Work at it. Set your jaw. Be determined that you will be the king God has chosen you to be.

I have used these scriptures as a foundation for my thinking and activity for years. I have gone over them and meditated on them. They are in my spirit. They are bringing me into new strengths and levels of growth in this kingly ministry.

"The soul of the sluggard desireth and hath nothing: but the soul of the diligent shall be made fat."

If you are so lazy that you cannot put forth some fight or some determination and effort then you will always be bringing up the tail.

The lazy man can only wish and desire. He cannot possess.

REIGN FINANCIALLY
BECAUSE IT IS GOD'S WILL

Deuteronomy 15:6-7 "For the Lord thy God blesseth thee, as he promised thee: and thou shalt lend unto many nations, but thou shalt not borrow; and thou shalt reign over many nations, but they shall not reign over thee. If there be among you a poor man of one of thy brethren within any of thy gates in thy land ... you shall not harden thine heart ... from thy poor brother."

1 Corinthians 15:25 "For he must reign, till he hath put all enemies under his feet."

"You shall lend unto many nations."

Israel was rich when she served God. She did not have to borrow. Solomon had an abundance of wealth. Other kings who made any attempt to serve the Lord were wealthy. They ruled over the surrounding countries. It was only when sin crept in that they began to lose their authority and their finances. God's perfect will for Israel was that they "Come to the place where there were no poor among them." They never accomplished this, but it was God's will for them.

In Jesus you are the real Israel. You are to have enough financial power to rule for Jesus in this life. Read Galatians 3:13-16. The real seed of Abraham was in the spirit. It was not

Israel in the flesh. The promises all went to his seed singular which is Christ. In Christ every promise to Abraham is yours.

You are to be successful financially. You are to reign over the money situation.

"You shall not borrow."

Israel never had to borrow when she moved in God. Individuals did from time to time, but this was in God's permissive will. You may have to borrow, but you will mature to the point that you will do this less and less.

I know some men who like to give all of their money into the gospel and then borrow for their next business venture. If God leads you this way, walk ye in it. The main thing, you are not to be a servant to the lender. Some people become slaves to their creditors. You shall not be in bondage to a credit card, dear one. Get rid of most of them if you cannot trust yourself.

DO NOT LET THE WICKED REIGN OVER YOU

Proverbs 19:10 "Delight is not seemly for a fool; much less for a servant to have rule over princes."

This Hebrew word for delight could also be translated luxury. Luxury is not right for a foolish man. He cannot handle it. Immature men have been ruling and reigning over situations too long. Fools have taken over countries or businesses. Fools too often control our nations.

You are the princes and kings who should be reigning over God's business. Little men have controlled churches and corporations too long.

Proverbs 29:2 "When the righteous are in authority, the people rejoice: but when the wicked beareth rule, the people mourn."

It is a great day when strong men of God rise and reign in the body of Christ. It is a wonderful hour when righteous men reign in politics.

Isaiah 3:4-5 "I will give children to be their princes, and babes shall rule over them. The people shall be oppressed, every one by another ... the child shall behave himself proudly against the ancient, and the base against the honourable."

It is a sad day when school children tell the authorities how to run the school.

It is a sad day when children riot in the streets to determine the destiny of a country. Many times these are controlled by a rabble rousing terrorist group.

It is a great day when God's children take their authority and rule over these situations.

Isaiah 3:12 "As for my people, children are their oppressors, and women rule

over them..."

When man lives for the pleasures of the flesh he is headed down. The rebellious spirit in women's lib may be part of this scripture also. Woe to the land when the women fill the larger leadership role.

SIN PERMITS THE ENEMY TO RULE OVER YOU

Leviticus 26:17 "I will set my face against you, and ye shall be slain before your enemies: they that hate you shall reign over you; and ye shall flee when none pursueth you."

Seek the Lord, and you are indestructible. Serve flesh, and you will flee when none pursueth.

Romans 6:12 "Let not sin therefore reign in your mortal body, that ye should obey it in the lusts thereof."

You are to reign over sin. Sin is not to reign over you. You have a choice.

TO REIGN YOU MUST MOVE WITH AUTHORITY AND CONFIDENCE

Matthew 7:29 "He taught them as one having authority..."

The authority is in you. The Word is to be released with confidence and authority. Get alone with the Lord and see yourself talking with others with power and authority. See your words coming forth with love and power. Let this be embedded in your spirit. You will begin to see this authority flowing out of you as Jesus had it flowing from Him.

REIGN BY WORDS OF FAITH

Matthew 8:8-9 "The centurion answered and said, Lord, I am not worthy that thou shouldest come under my roof: but speak the word only, and my servant shall be healed. For I am a man under authority, having soldiers under me: and I say to this man, go, and he goeth; and to another come, and he cometh..."

The centurion was accustomed to moving in authority. He was accustomed to giving commands and expecting them to be carried out. The blind beggar on the other hand only knew how to beg. Each man approached the Lord on his own level. The centurion got quicker results.

Visualize yourself speaking to diseases with authority. See yourself speaking to business situations with authority. When you have a negative result, do not give up. Keep pressing forward into your kingdom. See yourself as one who moves in authority. See yourself blessed in your kingdom.

DISCIPLES REIGNED BY JESUS' AUTHORITY

Luke 9:1 "Then he called his twelve disciples together, and gave them power

and authority over all devils, and to cure diseases."

In Luke 10 Jesus gave this authority to the seventy which he sent to preach and to heal. Later he gave it to every believer. Visualize yourself with this authority.

Meditate on this.

Come to the place where you believe this authority is working.

See it in your mind's eye. See yourself walking in this power and authority. Keep working on this. As you pray for people and situations, see this authority working. It will begin to manifest itself through your life.

REIGN BY HARMONY

It is important for the pistons of an automobile to harmonize in their firing order. The engine loses power if it is out of time. It is important for homes to be in harmony. It is impossible for the full authority to operate unless the two be agreed.

Matthew 18:18-19 "... Whatsoever ye shall bind on earth shall be bound in heaven ... if two of you shall agree ..."

Find someone with whom you can agree in prayer.

CHAPTER 4

REIGNING BY THE POWER OF GOD

GOD'S POWER IS CREATIVE

Jeremiah 10:12 "He hath made the earth by his power, he hath established the world by his wisdom, and hath stretched out the heavens by his discretion."

Jeremiah 10:13 "When he uttereth his voice, there is a multitude of waters in the heavens, and he causeth the vapours to ascend from the ends of the earth..."

"He hath made the earth by his power."

God's power flowing through your life is creative.

"He hath established the world by his wisdom."

God's power working in your life creates great ministries.

God's power working in your life creates great business empires.

God's power working in your life changes your home and community.

"When he uttereth his voice, there is a multitude..."

Things happen when the Lord speaks through your mouth. Lives are changed. Problems are settled. God's power is right there in your life waiting to be utilized by you.

SPIRIT WORDS IN YOUR MOUTH RELEASE THIS POWER

Acts 5:5 "Ananias hearing these words fell down, and gave up the ghost: and great fear came on all them that heard these things."

Peter had said to Ananias, "Why hath Satan filled thine heart to lie to the Holy Ghost, and to keep back part of the price of the land?"

Words of knowledge flowed forth from Peter's mouth. Miracles took place. The wicked church member was exposed. Ananias was struck dead.

Acts 5:11 "Great fear came upon all the church, and upon as many as heard these things."

The power of God caused the early church to be feared and respected from within and without.

This is a crucial time in the history of man. You, too, can cause respect and fear for the power of God to return to the ministry of the Lord Jesus Christ.

Acts 2:41 "They that gladly received his word were baptized ... about three thousand souls."

Three thousand souls were added to the church that day. God's power was so great through Peter's mouth that three thousand people repented and turned to Jesus Christ.

Luke 4:32 "... His word was with power."

Jesus' words flowing through you are with power. He is in the supernatural resurrection power right now. He is at the Father's right hand. He has more power today than when He was on earth. See yourself moving and speaking His words with power.

His words are healing people.

His words are creating financial miracles.

His words from your lips are setting the captives free.

Believe that you reign by using His words.

I have seen this over and over in our ministry. I expect to see an increase daily. The Lord will receive honor from me as I anticipate and release His power.

Acts 10:44 "While Peter yet spake these words, the Holy Ghost fell on all them

which heard the word."

In one form or another I have seen this same thing repeated often in our meetings. I have seen people who had sought the baptism of the Holy Ghost for thirty years receive immediately when the right spirit words were spoken to them.

One man was seeking the Holy Spirit. Seemingly he could not receive. I kept speaking to him, but it did not help. Then I stepped forward and whispered instructions to him from the Holy Spirit. The man acted on this. The power of God hit him. He did a backward flip and started speaking in tongues. At one moment he was locked, stiff, and stayed. As he responded to the words of the Lord, the stiff spirit left, and miracles followed. I have seen this literally hundreds of time in our ministry.

Romans 4:17 "... Even God, who quickeneth the dead, and calleth those things which be not as though they were."

God called and miracles took place.

God calls through your lips and things happen.

Some time back I ministered to a couple by prophecy. I told them that money would come to them for their project. It was not long after that that someone gave them five thousand dollars. They were able to start the project. Then in a few weeks ninety-five thousand dollars more was given to them. They are still rejoicing in the Lord.

I sat down and talked with a man a few years ago. As a result of that conversation his whole life was changed. He paid his bills. He bought a large farm and paid for it in a few years. Miracle after miracle began to work in his life.

Needless to say when I talk to people out of my soulish realm nothing supernatural happens. What a thrill it is to see God move and change people. We see this often enough to stay all excited about Jesus' miracle words flowing through our life.

1 Kings 17:1 "Elijah ... said ... As the Lord God of Israel liveth, before whom I stand, there shall not be dew nor rain these years, but according to my word."

Elijah said, "There will be no rain except that which I speak into existence before God." God put those words in his mouth. It did not rain for approximately three years. The same prophet had to release that rain, but it was God who did it through him. 1 Kings 18:1: "... *The word of the Lord came to Elijah in the third year, saying, Go, shew thyself unto Ahab; and I will send rain upon the earth.*"

1 Kings 17:13-14 "Elijah said unto her, Fear not; go and do as thou hast said: but make me thereof a little cake first, and

bring it unto me, and after make for thee and for thy son. For thus saith the Lord God of Israel, The barrel of meal shall not waste, neither shall the cruse of oil fail, until the day that the Lord sendeth rain upon the earth."

The woman obeyed the words of the Lord spoken by the prophet. There was a miracle flow of oil and meal. *"The barrel of meal wasted not, neither did the cruse of oil fail, according to the word of the Lord, which he spake by Elijah."* (1 Kings 17:16)

This was a very dramatic miracle. You have been used by God in the past. Perhaps it was not so dramatic, but you have been used. Anticipate this happening more often. This will increase as the day of the Lord approaches. Praise the Lord Jesus!

GOD IS YOUR POWER

2 Samuel 22:33 "God is my strength and power..."

Let God be your source. Do not look to your own achievements. Do not look to what you have been in the natural.

God's strength is flowing through your hands.

His strength is flowing through your eyes.

His strength is flowing through your mouth.

Visualize His power working through you

and changing your world. You are not alone. He is with you to perform His wonderful word.

2 Samuel 22:30 "By thee I have run through a troop: by my God have I leaped over a wall."

Visualize God's power flowing through you. See yourself running through every obstacle that blocks your path to victory. See yourself reigning in this life. You are leaping over that wall that the enemy has erected. Refer to this verse often. Make this your life. Arise and do exploits.

2 Samuel 22:35 "He teacheth my hands to war; so that a bow of steel is broken by mine arms."

David gave God credit for all of his victories. The anointing of God caused him to break steel with his hands. God's power caused the giant to fall to David. God's strength caused the lion and the bear to fall to David. God's power caused David's men to do exploits.

God's strength is still the same. It is flowing to you. You can release it. Visualize yourself moving in this strength. God is strong through you.

When you visualize yourself, visualize God's power and God's strength at your disposal. Do not back off in the corner and feel sorry for yourself. You have His strength.

Believe it as you meet today's challenge. See the bands that have kept you down broken by God's strength flowing out through your life.

OPERATE IN GOD'S POWER

2 Peter 1:3 "... His divine power hath given unto us all things that pertain unto life and godliness, through the knowledge of him..."

Ephesians 6:10 "... Be strong in the Lord, and in the power of his might."

His power has provided everything you need to function in supernatural miracles. You already have it. It is through the principles of Jesus Christ. "Knowledge of him" includes walking in His spirit. It includes positive faith. It includes the full principle of life in which Jesus operated while here on earth. Obedience is important. Prayer is important.

Set yourself today to be strong in every move you make. Set your jaw. Set your face like a flint. Refuse to budge. You will be strong right now in this life in God's power. See this power flowing freely. See yourself completely revolutionized from what you have been in the past.

1 Corinthians 4:20 "The kingdom of God is not in word, but in power."

Positive confession must not be presumption. It must flow from the spirit of God. The

Christian life is more than creeds or even as Jesus said, "Sacrifice."

God wants more than religion.

He wants more than teaching.

He wants reality.

He expects power.

Go beyond the itching-ear stage and step into reality. Produce the power that you already possess.

1 Corinthians 5:4 "In the name of our Lord Jesus Christ, when ye are gathered together, and my spirit, with the power of our Lord Jesus Christ."

Your power always flows from the name and authority of the Lord Jesus Christ. When two or three are gathered together in His name there is a multiple of power. He is present in a special way. His spirit is there. His power is there. Things happen when the saints gather together. *"Where two or three are gathered together in my name, there am I in the midst of them."* (Matthew 18:20)

Come expecting miracles. Come expecting answered prayers. Leave knowing that God has done something in a very special way each time you meet in Jesus' name.

Gear your thoughts to miracles, and changes will come to pass through the power of God in Jesus' name. Step out into this power flow and try to activate it. More and more you will find the key.

THE POWER OF GOD IS OFTEN RELEASED BY WEAK VESSELS

Psalm 8:2 "Out of the mouth of babes and sucklings hast thou ordained strength..."

Sucklings are still on milk. They are breast or bottle babies. They are not mature. Do not wait until you are mature, or you will be so stiff spiritually that you can not move in God.

Matthew 11:25 "...Thou hast hid these things from the wise and prudent, and hast revealed them unto babes."

Revelation knowledge comes to the tender hearts.. These may be young or old saints. They must be babes in heart. Truths are given to the tender, teachable saints. If you have it all figured out, then you will have to be satisfied with your present level. You are too smart to be taught. You must be teachable.

2 Corinthians 12:10 "...When I am weak, then am I strong."

An attitude of being weak in flesh but strong in spirit produces miracles. A stubborn flesh-will stops the flow of God. Obedience to spirit commands releases the power of God. Be submissive to His instructions.

One lady, in a prayer meeting, was so stubborn or fearful that she would not obey the spirit. The spirit told her to hit the table.

Three days later when she hit the table the power fell. Be tender enough to submit your will to Him.

During or immediately following a long fast of ten days or more I see more miracles than when I am well fed.

2 Corinthians 4:11 "For we which live are alway delivered unto death for Jesus' sake, that the life also of Jesus might be made manifest in our mortal flesh."

Those who suffer for their own ignorance, mistakes, or sins have no reward in this respect. If you are in a "jam" because of real Jesus actions, expect Jesus' miracles. Jesus will flow out of your life when you are up against a wall if you know how to press the faith button. When you come to an end of the fleshly ability and turn it over to Jesus, you will see results. Do not wait till you are in a jam to trust God.

If you are under persecution or other forms of pressures because of your life in Christ, right now start looking for the blessings. They are there for you right now.

1 Corinthians 2:3 "I was with you in weakness, and in fear, and in much trembling."

Step out in humility and reverence into your Jesus ministry.

1 Corinthians 2:5 "That your faith should

not stand in the wisdom of men, but in the power of God."

Miracles will flow when Godly fear is present in your heart. People about you or under your ministry will be established by the confirmation of the power of God and not by the teaching of the dead letter.

Numbers 12:3 "... Moses was very meek, above all the men which were upon the face of the earth."

Paul walked in weakness, fear, and trembling. Jesus walked in the spirit of meekness and gentleness. When you teach yourself to be meek and gentle, you are teaching yourself the route to power.

Psalm 149:4 "... He will beautify the meek with salvation."

Deliverance will flow to and through the tender, meek spirit. The road to power and authority is love, gentleness, meekness, and service.

Matthew 18:3 "... Except ye be converted and become as little children, ye shall not enter into the kingdom of heaven."

The hard spirit cannot hear the voice of God. He does not know when the spirit speaks. He is dull of hearing. He is calloused.

Train yourself to be as a little child. Do this by being gentle with all people. Step back and bless others. Fasting and prayer will help you here also. Giving of your finances to a needy person or cause will help.

POWER AND AUTHORITY
FLOW THROUGH HIS WORD

John 8:31-32 "... If ye continue in my word, then are ye my disciples indeed; and ye shall know the truth, and the truth shall make you free."

Walk in His word. When the word comes alive in your spirit, you are in the power of the Spirit.

I have seen many people delivered from demon spirits when they walked in truth by confessing their sins and loving their enemies. I have seen others delivered by shouting out, "I am free."

Jesus has set you free. Stand up and declare the truth. You are free. Now act like it.

John 17:17 "Sanctify them through thy truth: thy word is truth."

Sanctify means to make holy or to purify. God makes you holy and pure with His word. His word has power. It is power. It purifies. It heals. It blesses. It is God. *"The Word was God."* (John 1:1)

If you will stay with any truth long enough to believe it in your inner man, changes will take place in your life and personality.

John 15:7 "If ye abide in me, and my words abide in you, ye shall ask what ye will, and it shall be done unto you."

When you abide in Jesus you ask what the spirit prompts you to ask. Abiding in him implies walking in the spirit. It is not presumption. It is not the work of a novice. It is living in the Jesus life and principle.

According to Strong, *ask* could mean to beg, ask, call for, crave, desire, or require. Actually the spirit is calling for the thing through you. The spirit is asking for it, but your desire and mouth are cooperating with Him. "It is God which worketh in you, both to will and to do of his good pleasure." God is praying through you. God is beseeching or begging through you. *"Likewise the Spirit also helpeth our infirmities: for we know not what we should pray for as we ought: but the spirit itself maketh intercession for us with groanings which cannot be uttered . . . he maketh intercession for the saints according to the will of God."* (Romans 8:26-27)

The word of God provides the atmosphere and elements which cause faith to work in and through you.

1 Peter 1:23 "Being born again, not of corruptible seed, but of incorruptible, by the word of God which liveth and abideth for ever."

I was saved by standing on John 1:12 and

John 3:16. That word brought the power of God to my life. It brought salvation to my life. I never backslid once after that. The Word brought the nature of God to my life. *"Whereby are given unto us exceeding great and precious promises: that by these ye might be partaker of the divine nature . . ."* (2 Peter 1:4)

James 1:18 "Of his own will begat he us with the word of truth . . ."

God fathers you with the Word. When that living word makes contact with your spirit, God is joined to you. Let this living word make contact with you on different levels. Let the living word heal you, prosper you, give you favor, give you growth, give you fame and bring your entire personality into full maturity.

James 1:21 " . . . Receive with meekness the engrafted (implanted) word, which is able to save your souls."

Power is in that Word. It changes you. It saves your entire person. These people were born again. Saving the soul here by usage implies the saving of the whole man.

Hebrews 1:3 " . . . Upholding all things by the word of his power . . ."

Everything in heaven and earth is fully controlled by the word that flows from the Father. As you yield to that word and speak it by the Holy Ghost, you are yielding into the highest power in existence.

This word flows continually to you. The Bible is that word. This word will also flow directly to you. The Spirit may quicken the written word to you, or He may speak a fresh word to you. None of it will be contrary to the principles of the proven, written word.

Hebrews 11:3 "... The worlds were framed by the word of God..."

Psalm 33:6 & 9 "By the word of the Lord were the heavens made; and all the host of them by the breath of his mouth. For he spake, and it was done; he commanded, and it stood fast."

Everything must respond to that word from the Father. Jesus yielded to these words and the worlds were created. He yielded and the sick were cleansed. You yield to them, and you too will have miracles. Visualize yourself moving in the power of this wonderful word.

I often say if a person moves in love and exercises wisdom, sooner or later, he will speak God's word. I usually have enough words going that some of them are bound to be from the Holy Ghost.

POWER COMES WITH THE HOLY GHOST

Acts 1:8 "Ye shall receive power after that the Holy Ghost is come upon you: and ye shall be witnesses unto me..."

One lady said to me, "I have received the Holy Spirit, now where is the power?"

You have the power. Walk in it. Expect it to happen. Everything works by faith.

I have found a dramatic change in my witness since receiving the Holy Spirit. I walk in more confidence. I walk in love. I look at people with love and compassion and in this atmosphere, speak the word of the Lord to them. Each witness is different. God deals differently with each one.

You need to know that you have this power if you have received the baptism of the Holy Ghost. Each of you has your calling and your witness will reflect this calling. Many of you should see yourself bringing people into strong churches. Find a strong church for yourself and then bring people into that church with you. Go out and compel them to come into the body of Christ. Lead them to Christ if you can, and then take them to church with you. Entice them by taking them to dinner with you after church. Get something constructive working. Utilize this power. This power also includes healing miracles in the physical body and in home situations.

You have this power.

Know that you have this power.

Act like you have this power. Walking around disbelieving this power blocks God from moving through you. Deep down inside act like you are the only person in the world who has this power. This will help you release it yourself rather than leaning on another.

Last night during service a boy came up to me with a sickness. He talked for a while and went to another group of saints for a few moments. I went about my business of dealing with others. Soon he came back alive with excitement. He said, "I was about to have you pray for my sickness, but one of the saints said, 'let us pray.' They did. I am healed." Yes, you can pray the prayer of faith.

Visualize yourself moving in Holy Ghost power. See people being helped by your words and by your prayers. Have a happy, content feeling about your ministry. This gives you confidence and courage to get the job done.

Acts 6:5 "... They chose Stephen, a man full of faith and of the Holy Ghost."

Acts 6:8 "Stephen, full of faith and power, did great wonders and miracles..."

There is little record of Stephen moving in this power until he accepted the responsibility. Once he fully accepted that he had the power, it seemed to surface more and more.

You too will recognize changes in your ministry and effectiveness in Holy Ghost power when you make up your mind that you can do it too. Get off the side line and get involved.

Acts 10:38 "How God anointed Jesus of Nazareth with the Holy Ghost and with power: who went about doing good, and healing all that were oppressed of the devil; for God was with him."

Jesus Christ still is anointed with power. Jesus Christ flowing through you is still anointed to go about doing good. God is still with him. You can stop crying about not having a ministry. Start using the power that abides in you. It will soon activate, and you will be so busy you will not know yourself.

Stop long enough to see Jesus flowing out through you to others about you. Do this several times during the day. Cultivate love and compassion for those about you as you visualize Christ reaching out to them through you. Sometimes you will not say a word to them. Jesus' love will flow out silently to them. He is working in them.

Zechariah 4:6 " . . . Not by might, nor by power, but by my spirit, saith the Lord of hosts."

His spirit flowing in the earth is powerful. His spirit flowing through you is powerful.

Micah 3:8 "But truly I am full of power by the spirit of the Lord, . . ."

Repeat this often to yourself. You are full

of power by the spirit of the Lord. You can do miracles. You are doing miracles. Changes are happening in your life and your outreaches in business. Your family is changing as this power continues to flow. People's attitudes toward you are changing as you see your usefulness. When you see yourself as valuable, others will see the same thing.

THIS POWER IS IN JESUS' NAME

You have lost your earth identity. You now operate in your heavenly family authority and name. It is like the bride. She loses her maiden name and takes on her husband's family name. You now have the name of the Lord Jesus Christ. It is God's redemptive name. It is the power that all hell recognizes.

Ephesians 1:21 "Far above all principality, and power, and might, and dominion, and every name that is named, not only in this world, but also in that which is to come."

There is no name higher than that name.

Philippians 2:9-10 "Wherefore God also hath highly exalted him, and given him a name which is above every name: That at the name of Jesus every knee should bow, of things in heaven, and things in earth, and things under the earth."

Every demon must respond to that name. Every problem you have must respond to that name.

Every sickness must respond to that name.

You should know the power of that name. The power of His name is activated when you truly believe. Presumption will not get the job done. It has to be absolute confidence in the power and authority of that name. I have found that it usually comes when I stop trying and relax and simply trust the Lord to honor His name.

EVERY BELIEVER HAS THIS POWER

Luke 10:19 "Behold, I give unto you power to tread on serpents and scorpions, and over all the power of the enemy: and nothing shall by any means hurt you."

Mark 16:17-18 "These signs shall follow them that believe; In my name shall they cast out devils; they shall speak with new tongues; they shall take up serpents; and if they drink any deadly thing, it shall not hurt them; they shall lay hands on the sick, and they shall recover."

Hebrews 2:6-8 "... What is man, that thou art mindful of him? or the son of man, that thou visitest him? Thou madest him a little lower than the angels; thou crownedst him with glory and honour, and didst set him over the works of thy hands: Thou hast put all things in subjec-

tion under his feet..."

Matthew 17:20 "... If ye have faith ... nothing shall be impossible unto you."

You have power to tread on serpents. You have power over all the power that Satan could throw against you. Stop running from your problems. Stop and face them in Jesus' name. They will begin to fall at your commands.

In Jesus' name you will cast out devils. You will do exploits. People will recover when you pray. Start praying. Do not worry about the casualties. When you pray for enough people some of them are bound to believe. This will encourage you. More and more your percentage of success will increase. Soon you will be in a great deliverance ministry.

"Thou hast made him a little lower than the angels."

In Psalm 8:5 where this verse is found, the Hebrew word for angels was God. God made man just a little lower than God himself.

You are crowned with glory and honor.

You are a miracle worker.

You are over His ministry.

You are in charge of your own success.

All powers are subject to you.

CHAPTER 5

THE VALUE OF OBEDIENCE IN REIGNING

> Romans 15:3 "... Christ pleased not himself..."
>
> John 6:38 "I came down from heaven, not to do mine own will, but the will of him that sent me."

Jesus was conscious of the Father's will for His life. He strove to please the Father in everything. Any need alerted Him to be obedient to the Father. When He got that little nudge He stepped forth and obeyed the Father's commands. He assures us in John 5:19 that He never stepped out in presumption of the flesh or soulish realm. *"The Son can do nothing of himself, but what he seeth the Father do: for what things soever he doeth, these also doeth the Son likewise."*

Be ready to please the Lord. Be alert.

The world is full of opportunities for you to exercise your ministry. Step out and develop your faith.

Recently I stepped out of a motel room. A man next to me was grinding away on his starter trying to get his automobile started. It would not start. He had been working for some time. He had his hood lifted and had been fooling around here and there. I stepped over to see if I could help. He gave me some sort of an excuse why it would not start. He said there isn't much we can do. I laid my hands on the fender and said, "Jesus, let it start," and walked away without saying anything else.

I was in my car backing from the curb when he came running. He said, "She is running. You can lay hands on me any time you want."

Praise the Lord. Jesus got the glory. That man will not forget that for a long time.

Be ready to please Jesus. You are not here to do your own will but the will of Him that sent you. Picture Jesus walking in you today doing exciting things to a lot of nice people about you.

PEOPLE WILL BE BLESSED
WHEN YOU OBEY THE LORD

Genesis 22:18 "In thy seed shall all the nations of the earth be blessed; because thou hast obeyed my voice."

Genesis 26:4-5 "I will make thy seed to multiply as the stars of heaven, and will

give unto thy seed all these countries; and in thy seed shall all the nations of the earth be blessed; because that Abraham obeyed my voice, and kept my charge, my commandments, my statutes, and my laws."

"All the nations of the earth" refers primarily to the Gentiles coming to Jesus through Abraham's obedience and faith. Abraham stepped out and did what God commanded. He could have stayed back home where things were smooth. He did not do this. He responded to the call of the Lord.

There was to be a blessing upon his own life. His seed would multiply as the stars of heaven. All of this happened because Abraham obeyed the Lord.

Things happen when you obey God.

Recently when I was in a motel room, I asked the maid something about the Lord, and then without hesitation I prayed for her. She was saved. Later she came back and said, "Tell me again what you did to me for I feel so good." Later that evening she called my room from her home and wanted to know more about Jesus.

Today my wife and I were here in this motel where I am writing this manuscript. The maid was making up the bed. Her hand was all swollen and crooked. She had caught it in a sheet while it was in the dryer. This had necessitated several operations on her hand

and she was going the next day for another operation. I took her hand without even asking her if she wanted me to pray and asked the Lord to take care of that hand.

I do not believe she will need further surgery. Praise the Lord Jesus.

Deuteronomy 11:26-28 ". . . I set before you this day a blessing and a curse; A blessing, if ye obey the commandments of the Lord your God, which I command you this day: And a curse, if ye will not obey the commandments of the Lord your God, but turn aside out of the way which I command you . . ."

So often the children of Israel turned aside to other gods after they had enjoyed a long period of prosperity. The flesh keeps calling you to submit to its enticements.

When Israel obeyed God there were always blessings beyond words.

Prosperity was present in abundance.

Peace with their neighbors was present to the fullest.

Health was everywhere.

It was only when they began to disobey God that trouble came to them. The enemy would rise up. Sickness would come.

God does not change. It is the same today. Jesus said to the lame man in John 5:14: *"Behold, thou art made whole: sin no more, lest a worse thing come unto thee."*

Sin seemingly opens the door, and Satan comes with his disease, poverty, destruction, etc.

The people, due to sin, were overthrown in the desert in the Old Testament. Paul said, *"Now these things were our examples, to the intent we should not lust after evil things, as they also lusted . . . neither let us commit fornication, as some of them committed, and fell in one day three and twenty thousand. Neither let us tempt Christ, as some of them also tempted, and were destroyed of serpents. Neither murmur ye, as some of them also murmured, and were destroyed of the destroyer. Now all of these things happened unto them for ensamples: and they are written for our admonition, upon whom the ends of the world are come."* (1 Corinthians 10:6-11)

The Old Testament is given to us as examples of God's operations.

"I set before you a blessing and a curse, a blessing if ye obey the commandments of the Lord . . ."

You are a blessing everywhere you go. You do love God. You do obey God. People's lives are being changed. You are a man or woman of God. God is in you. You are carrying miracles around with you. A blessing is set before you. God is blessing you and others. You control your own destiny. You also influence the destiny of those about you.

Recently I met a woman who had an appointment with her physician to have her finger operated on the very next day. I said, "Wait, let me minister to you." Then I said, "Be healed in Jesus' name." We talked faith after this. I told her I did not believe she would need the operation. She went to the doctor as scheduled. He said, "This has improved so much I will not have to operate." She came back the next day shouting and giving God all the credit.

You can be a blessing to those about you, or you can hold your peace. The latter will result in their not being delivered. This amounts to being a curse to them. You could have helped them if you had released the power of God.

Recently my wife and I prayed for a lady who could not straighten one of her finger joints from birth. Buddy (my wife) and I prayed, and instantly she shouted, "I can straighten it! Look!" She was healed right there.

We were a blessing to her. If we had held our peace, we would have in one sense been a curse to her. We not only blessed her, but we blessed ourselves as well. When you give, then God and men give to you. Blessings flow to those who bless others. You can bless yourself or curse yourself by obeying or disobeying the Lord. He is wonderful, and you are great yourself. Fall in love with Jesus.

Fall in love with the Christ who is in you. Smile and go about doing good. You have a great ministry. Yes, you are truly a blessing to people this day.

PROSPERITY COMES WHEN YOU OBEY THE LORD

Isaiah 1:19-20 "If ye be willing and obedient, ye shall eat the good of the land: but if ye refuse and rebel, ye shall be devoured with the sword: for the mouth of the Lord hath spoken it."

James 4:8 "Draw nigh to God, and he will draw nigh to you . . ."

The man who is led by the Spirit is the real son of God.

You are beginning to learn the principles of the faith walk. You are drawing nigh to the Lord. He is blessing you. You can look about and see the good of the land flowing to you.

Go beyond what you see now and see a greater portion of prosperity coming your way. You are not through yet. Your ministry has not yet climaxed. Reach out for a real breakthrough.

You *are* willing.

You *are* obedient.

You are eating the good of the land.

Develop this attitude. Good things are moving your way. God's blessings are coming your way.

Obedience is important. One phase of obedience is believing what He has said. He has said, *"If ye be willing and obedient, ye shall eat the good of the land."*

Believe this.

See changes coming to you.

See yourself important in the kingdom of God.

See yourself reigning.

You *are* obedient.

Any self-condemnation spirit must go. Away with it. Any spirit that says you cannot do it must go. You must be obedient to see yourself strong in Jesus. Get up now and produce.

OBEDIENCE, NOT RELIGION, IS THE KEY

1 Samuel 15:22-23 ". . . To obey is better than sacrifice, and to hearken than the fat of rams. For rebellion is as the sin of witchcraft, and stubbornness is as iniquity and idolatry. . ."

Jesus said, *"I will have mercy, and not sacrifice..."* (Matthew 12:7) Religion and its works do not satisfy the Lord. Fasting and praying in themselves do not satisfy the Lord. God wants your heart full of love and sincerity. The Holy Spirit will give you much work to do, but He must do the motivating.

Saul disobeyed the voice of the Lord and kept the sheep for religious purposes. He kept King Agag for soulish reasons. For this act of rebellion his kingdom was rent from him. *"Because thou hast rejected the word of the Lord, he hath also rejected thee from being king."*

You are to lay aside *"Every weight, and the sin which doth so easily beset us..."* (Hebrews 12:1) Little acts of disobedience many times destroy quicker than major sins.

"To obey is better than sacrifice."

Obedience to the words of faith given by the Holy Ghost is the only way to reign in this life. One act of obedience may bring miracles where days of prayer may not. On other occasions the Spirit may lead you to days of prayer and praise. Obedience is the key.

Learning to step out and act on Spirit nudges is very important. Being ready for the Spirit to move at all times is important. It may be when you are in line at the grocery store. It may be in the midst of a business transaction. Be ready to act on Spirit commands. This is a fun key. It is also exciting.

There have been times when I started moving in the Spirit before I even started preaching and God saved sinners and filled people with the Holy Ghost.

Buddy (my wife) received a word from God warning of an accident. She moved in obedience and rebuked the accident. Later that same day as we were driving on the highway we saw the result of that prayer. God saved a child from getting hit by another car.

A friend of mine had a bad water pump on her car. It had gone bad in a city far from her home. The garages were closed. In obedience to the command of the Lord, she told the filling station attendant to fill it with water. He did it under protest. She drove the car for two years after this. She told the man who bought the car about this incident and he laughed and scoffed at her. The water pump went out on the way home and the man ruined the engine. To try it out, he had driven the car for three days while she still owned the car. The pump did not leak then. As long as it was her car it worked. When unbelief took over the ownership of the car the miracle ceased.

The same lady ruined her own car a few years later. It had overheated. She stepped out in front of the car and shouted. "Hallelujah, I will be better off. God will work this out for my good. Satan meant it for evil, but God will get good out of this." The car had 55,000 miles on it. All warranties were long gone. The car dealer favored her and put in a new motor free of all charges.

Obedience is a very important key.

One thing is certain. God does not like groanings, grumblings, and complainings. He likes joyful saints. Maintain the victory at all times even when you feel like crying. Laugh at your situation and praise the Lord. You too will be better off because of this act of faith and obedience.

Deuteronomy 1:27 "Ye murmured in your tents, and said, because the Lord hated us, he hath brought us forth out of the land of Egypt, to deliver us into the hand of the Amorites, to destroy us."

The Lord heard their murmurings and their rebellions and would not let them go into the promised land. *"The Lord heard the voice of your words, and was wroth, and sware, saying, surely there shall not one of these men of this evil generation see that good land..."* (Deuteronomy 1:34-35)

I have developed a strong positive attitude when trouble strikes. Occasionally I fail momentarily in the midst of the pressure, but I am gaining strength even in this. I see the victory before it ever arrives. I see *"The Lord ... going before me, he shall fight for me, according to all that he did for Israel..."* (Deuteronomy 1:30) I changed that verse from the second person to the first person.

In the midst of trouble I stop and visualize the end result. I see the Lord moving in and making the crooked places straight. Oh, this is the fun way to operate. Obedience to believe God for the victory is important.

"To obey is better than sacrifice."

If you are to reign in the gifts of the spirit

you must learn to obey the guidance of the Holy Spirit. I cannot repeat this too often. You must learn to step out and obey the Lord.

Look for the Spirit to move. Expect Him to move. Act on what He tells you to do. The Spirit speaks with a still, small voice most of the time. Keep tender to His voice. The impression may be slight. You may confuse it with your own soulish will. Work with the Lord. He will help you to develop.

God opened the door for me to take a 1300-mile trip to preach a revival. This was shortly after I received the Holy Spirit. I did not have much money. My car was old and the tires were bald. My 12-year-old daughter received a vision of Jesus driving our car to that distant city. We obeyed the Lord. Buddy and I laid our Holy Ghost hands on those tires, each one of them, and confessed that we would arrive without a flat. We did just that. We laid our hands on the ten dollars (all that we had for the trip) and said we would arrive without begging or telling folks of our need. We arrived with three dollars left over. The car gave supernatural gas mileage on the way there. Coming back it was back to normal. He blessed us financially in that meeting so we did not need the supernatural gas mileage. People were saved in that meeting. Many of those Baptists, 28 in all, received the Holy Ghost.

Many times when Buddy and I are ministering together in a service something she does will be a signal for me to make another move in the Holy Spirit. Great things follow these acts of obedience.

CHAPTER 6

WAITING ON GOD — A PREREQUISITE TO REIGNING

THERE IS A SEASON FOR EVERY SEED TO PRODUCE

Some seeds have a faster maturing season than others. Some mature in weeks. Others mature in years. You cannot compare your life with someone else's life. God will move in one person slower than another. Some people are ready for God to use them sooner. Others move slower into their more productive ministry because they need a tough preparation period prior to launching into the difficult areas in which they will walk.

Exodus 23:30 "By little and little I will drive them out from before thee, until thou be increased, and inherit the land."

God could not let them possess the land too rapidly. They could not handle it. You cannot move into your greater ministry ahead of your schedule. You may "blow" it.

The butterfly builds strength as it is breaking out of its cocoon. If you help it by tearing apart the cocoon, the butterfly will soon die. You must wait for your season.

Psalm 145:15 "The eyes of all wait upon thee; and thou givest them their meat in due season."

Wait on it. There is a due season for you. Do not push so fast that you get ahead of your own ability to handle it. You must balance your pushing and pressing forward with your waiting on God.

I know in my own life I have had to press forward by prayer, fasting, Bible study, and action. I have tried to step forward into every opportunity that came my way. I waited on the Lord as I pressed forward.

This same principle is still operating in my ministry. I keep pressing forward and at the same time I wait for God to move and bring things together.

Psalm 1:2-3 "His delight is in the law of the Lord; and in his law doth he meditate day and night. He shall be like a tree planted by the rivers of water, that bringeth forth his fruit in his season; his leaf also shall not wither; and whatsoever he doeth shall prosper."

First, you delight in His Word. You meditate on His Word continually. You will grow and become strong like a tree planted by the rivers of water. You will then bring forth your fruit in your proper season. You will not fail. Your leaf will not wither. You will prosper in your ministry.

Stay steady. Do not jump out into full-time ministry too fast. You can mess your family up doing this. If you want to preach, step into every open door, but keep your head. Keep your job. If you get to spending too much time preaching, and the finances are coming in, then you might pray about stepping out into full time. This will be true in most cases, but it is not necessarily true in every case. God may work completely opposite for you. Learn to obey God the best you can.

There is a season for greater breakthroughs within your ministry.

Hold steady.

Do not be discouraged.

Imagine yourself in your new level of reigning. See yourself as you will be in the new level. In your mind always see yourself beyond where you are. Have goals and move toward those goals as you wait for the proper opportunity or doors to open.

WAIT IN PATIENCE
FOR YOUR NEW REALM

Psalm 37:7 "Rest in the Lord, and wait patiently for him..."

Snuggle up to the Lord in absolute comfort on each level of growth. Know and have confidence in His timing and His interest in your case. Let this rest completely ease all anxiety or frustration.

God is near.

He cares.

He knows the sparrows. He surely knows about you.

God kept me down for two years after I received the Baptism of the Holy Spirit. I really wanted to get moving. God would not let me go to work during this time. I would get small, short-time jobs, but primarily it was waiting patiently by study and prayer. In the evenings we would go to teaching sessions in various churches. I knew things would open up some day. I did not try to rock the boat too much. Soon it happened. God began to move on my behalf. Doors began to open and they have been gradually swinging wider and wider ever since.

Psalm 40:1-2 "I waited patiently for the Lord; and he inclined unto me, and heard my cry. He brought me up also out of an horrible pit, out of the miry clay, and set my feet upon a rock, and established my goings."

Your day is coming.

He hears your prayer.

He is moving you out of that pit of despair.

Nothing can hold you back.

There was a time in my ministry when I had

to stand and declare that every door was open. The very next day after this God sent a prophet by and gave confirmation on this step of faith. In two weeks the doors began to open. When God does finally begin to move, things often happen quickly.

There are levels. You sail along on this new level for a while; then you have to dig in again. You start to seek God all over again for a new breakthrough. In its time it comes.

You may have to keep doing extra things during this time to help things happen. I have been working on books, radio, and television to help make things fall in place. Little by little God begins to work with you, and soon you walk out on a new level of faith ministry.

This is the basic operation for anything, whether it is a business, marriage, preaching ministry, or something else. You do something in faith. God moves. You wait. God moves some more and you must wait again, etc.

WAITING FOR YOUR REALM IN RIGHTEOUSNESS

Psalm 37:34 "Wait on the Lord, and keep his way, and he shall exalt thee to inherit the land..."

Stay close to Jesus. Do not let yourself become lazy. Discouragement is a sin that gets many folks during these levels of their reign. They want things to happen yesterday.

Keep a righteous spirit flowing out of your being. Do not allow yourself to grow soft and turn to the luxuries of the flesh life. Stay hungry for God. Practice fasting at least for short periods of time.

PERSISTENT WAITING

Job 13:15 "Though he slay me, yet will I trust in him: . . ."

No pressure can stop you from moving to your new place in this realm.
You have set your face like a flint.
You will not be moved.
You are going through.
Always see yourself there. You will soon be there.

WAIT, KNOWING THE ANSWER IS ON ITS WAY

Psalm 123:1-2 "Unto thee lift I up mine eyes, O thou that dwellest in the heavens. Behold, as the eyes of servants look unto the hand of their masters, and as the eyes of a maiden unto the hand of her mistress; so our eyes wait upon the Lord our God, until that he have mercy upon us."

The eyes of the servant look to the master for a reward. You are to be constantly looking to the Lord for a blessing. He teaches you here to expect Him to move. When you live expecting, the Lord will come. This is faith in action.

Jesus taught this same principle. *"And ye yourselves like unto men that wait for their lord, when he will return from the wedding; that when he cometh and knocketh, they may open unto him immediately. Blessed are those servants, whom the lord when he cometh shall find watching: verily I say unto you, that he shall gird himself, and make them to sit down to meat, and will come forth and serve them."* (Luke 12:36-37) Peter then asked the Lord if this pertained to the disciples or others. Jesus then said, *"Who then is that faithful and wise steward, whom his lord shall make ruler over his household, to give them their portion of meat in due season? Blessed is that servant, whom his lord when he cometh shall find so doing."* (Luke 12:42-43)

The answer to Peter's question lets us know it is for anyone of any dispensation. It may have been the disciples. It could have been any saint of any age. It will certainly pertain to the coming of the Lord in the end time. It applies to you right now.

You must live expecting something good to happen. Live knowing that Jesus has heard your prayer. He will soon be there. Discouragement or doubts will cause your level of expectancy to drop and will block the Lord from getting through to you. Unbelief stops God.

Many times the Lord has come to reward

His servants and found that they have left their post to attend to lesser duties of the flesh life. May God have mercy. How many times has the Lord come for you and not found you waiting?

WAIT AS A WATCHMAN THROUGH THE DARK NIGHT

Psalm 130:6 "My soul waiteth for the Lord more than they that watch for the morning: I say, more than they that watch for the morning."

Sometimes a person may be watching through the long night wishing for and even trying to rush the morning. Many times a person who is sick gets much worse during those night hours so he who is waiting longs for the morning to come. He knows dawn is coming but sometimes it seems that it will never arrive.

Then there is that watchman who is waiting during the night, waiting for the morning to arrive when all will be getting up and his vigil will be over. You are to watch knowing the morning will soon come. You are to watch knowing that you must hang in there till the dawn arrives. People are expecting you to watch over them and bring them through to safety.

You are responsible for others. They need your faithfulness to bring them safely through. You are to develop your ministry even though you have to wait faithfully through the long night.

WAIT IN FAITH

Psalm 27:13-14 "I had fainted, unless I had believed to see the goodness of the Lord in the land of the living. Wait on the Lord: be of good courage, and he shall strengthen thine heart: wait, I say, on the Lord."

Giving up before the blessing arrives is a common mistake. Hang in there. See yourself finishing every job you start. Set goals and carry them through to victory.

It is important that you see the answer before you start. See the finished product. Jesus spoke of first sitting down and counting the costs to determine if the job could be finished.

Believe that you are coming through to victory though it tarries.

As you wait, be sure to encourage yourself. Tell yourself that you are coming through to the full manifestation of your intention. Encourage yourself by visualizing yourself going through all frustrations. Know that the Lord is going before you to fight your battles. You are now actively believing. As you begin to believe first, then you produce the thing for which you are praying.

It is when you face your situation with courage, enthusiasm and joy that God strengthens you. God then begins to function on your behalf. The principle of God is that you believe first. You encourage yourself before you see the results.

WAIT FOR YOUR SUPERNATURAL MINISTRY

Isaiah 8:17-18 "I will wait upon the Lord, that hideth his face from the house of Jacob, and I will look for him. Behold, I and the children whom the Lord hath given me are for signs and for wonders in Israel from the Lord of hosts, which dwelleth in mount Zion."

God was hiding His face from Israel at this time because of their sin and rebellion. God does pull back when sin is present.

You and Jesus are God's children who have one purpose in being here. You are a sign and a wonder. Set your mind on that. Be assured that you are to have miracles in your life. This is your responsibility.

Begin to change all attitudes concerning yourself and the enemy. Take off your boxing gloves and use some brass knuckles in dealing with attitudes that push you back in the corner.

Stop all foolishness that short-circuits the power of God. Learn to train all thoughts into victorious channels.

WAIT FOR A NEW THRUST IN YOUR MINISTRY

Isaiah 40:29-31 "He giveth power to the faint; and to them that have no might he increaseth strength. Even the youths shall faint and be weary, and the young men shall utterly fall: But they that wait upon the Lord shall renew their strength; they shall mount up with wings as eagles; they shall run, and not be weary; and they shall walk, and not faint."

"He giveth power to the faint."

The hungry receive from God. They receive because they show hunger and desire.
Cultivate a receiving spirit.
Seek the Lord.
Enter into attitudes of prayer and fasting.
Stay up into the night until the physical becomes tired.

"To them that have no might he increaseth strength."

Always visualize an increase. When your spirit can see an increase it will come. The person who can visualize an increase has already decided there is a lack in his life. If your life hasn't produced the full resurrection ministry of Jesus Christ, there is a need. Comparing your life with that of Christ reveals you have a need.

"They that wait upon the Lord shall renew their strength."

Jumping out ahead of the Lord will get you in trouble. You may marry the wrong person doing this. You may make the wrong business deal. On the other hand, as you learn to flow in the spirit you will come up with right answers. Strength will flow.

Visualize yourself making the right deals all of the time.

"They shall mount up with wings as eagles."

The eagle flies high above the storm. You are reigning in this life by waiting for the flow of the spirit to direct you above the storms.

Your life is a life of strength.

It is a life of prosperity.

You have no limitations.

You are the head.

You are not a barnyard chicken who cannot clear even small fences.

Go high in your reign.

See yourself going beyond everything you have ever visualized for your life. Then make it come to pass as you submit to the spirit flow.

You never give up or submit to your present situation. Things may be falling apart all around you. You may be tempted to give up in despair.

Do not do it.

Rest.

Relax.

You can bring your life through the storm. God is with you. You have God-power in you through Jesus Christ. Never think of submitting to the level on which you are now walking. Go farther, man of God. Go beyond. Your eagle wings will take you where you were born to go.

Wait for it though it tarry.

CHAPTER 7

REIGNING BY STEPPING THROUGH OPEN DOORS

Closed doors have stopped many kings from reigning.

Personality problems close doors.

Laziness closes doors.

Lack of wisdom closes doors.

Failing to take advantage of the situation may close doors.

Fear to step out by faith in any particular area may be closing doors for you.

Many ideas that the spirit has given have been neglected. These are doors that will never be opened unless you learn to respond and act on them.

God is speaking to you.

Learn to listen.

Do not be dull of hearing.

GOD WILL CREATE OPEN DOORS FOR YOU

Genesis 21:19 "God opened her eyes, and she saw a well of water; and she

went, and filled the bottle with water, and gave the lad drink."

I do not know if God created this well for Hagar or not. It may have been that it was there all the time and she had overlooked it. God will create open doors for you. He will create situations through which you may walk to victory, or He may open your eyes to situations that you have overlooked. Either way, God will provide an answer in your situation.

Get this in your spirit.

God is on your side.

Look for that opportunity for which you have been waiting. Then walk in that open door.

SEE YOUR DOORS OPEN

Psalm 118:19 "Open to me the gates of righteousness: I will go into them, and I will praise the Lord."

A victorious attitude is important. God wants to open those doors for you. He wants to create unique situations for you. He loves you. He cares for you. He is opening the gates of righteousness.

It is important that you do not hesitate and miss God. You must walk through those gates at the opportune time.

For you to constantly visualize the door of opportunity closed against you only jams the door tighter. This would be working against yourself and against God. Cooperate with God. His word plainly declares that you are to be positive about this. The prayer of the psalmist was, *"Open to me the gate..."* Jesus said, *"When you pray, believe that you receive it."* Believe this gate or opportunity is open. It is. It will soon be manifested.

LACK OF WISDOM CLOSES THE DOOR OF OPPORTUNITY THAT GOD HAS OPENED

Psalm 78:23 "... Opened the doors of heaven."

Psalm 78:24 "... Had given them the corn of heaven."

Psalm 78:25 "... He sent them meat to the full."

Psalm 78:29 "So they did eat, and were filled..."

Psalm 78:30-31 "They were not estranged from their lust. But while their meat was yet in their mouths, the wrath of God came upon them..."

Fleshly operations close the doors of opportunity. Unwise decisions short-circuit the power of God. The doors of heaven may open as in these scriptures, corn from heaven may fall upon you, you may have eaten and been filled, but unless you move under God's Spirit and attitude you can lose it all. Unwise operations cause men to do many foolish and hurtful things to themselves.

You have seen people who would lose every dollar given to them by unwise decisions in business or childish spending of their money.

Determine that you will not squander the blessings God has given you by unwise decisions or carnal desires of the flesh.

GOD IS OPENING THE HEART DOORS OF OTHERS TO YOU

Acts 16:14 "A certain woman named Lydia, a seller of purple, of the city of Thyatira, which worshipped God, heard us: whose heart the Lord opened, that she attended unto the things which were spoken of Paul."

You have something the people need. Lydia needed the message Paul was speaking. You have a message of salvation that people need to hear. You have a business deal that certain other business people need to hear.

You can open your own doors or close them. A negative attitude will close the hearts which need to hear you. Go forth knowing that the right hearts will open to your message. Do not be discouraged if some do not open. Enough will open to make it worth your time.

A good way to get people to open their hearts to you is for you to open your heart to people. Selfishness will show through your front. This will scream louder than words. Be genuine through and through. Love people.

Whether you are preaching Jesus to a needy person or selling your business idea, visualize people receiving your message. See them loving you and receiving your presentation.

A suspicious spirit on your part will close more doors than you can open. Jesus speaks of *"mercy and not sacrifice."* You can fast and pray. You can be very religious. You can move by faith in some areas, but if you do not learn to be merciful and loving to yourself and to others there will be no reigning in your life. It is essential for you to have a healthy love and respect for yourself and your ability. It is equally important for you to love and appreciate your fellow man. He may not live up to your expectation as a person, but you still must love him and look beyond his shortcomings.

I know a woman who is very attractive. She is also very studious, but she is constantly struggling to get doors open. Her suspicion of people causes her to distrust them. Nearly every project she starts ends in disaster. Every friend soon turns and becomes an enemy.

See yourself loving people. See even your enemies as friends. Jesus Christ in you can change you and them. Occasionally you will find those who cannot be reached. Demonic personalities are still crucifying Jesus. You must look beyond this and minister to those with whom God has given you favor. He has many hearts that are open to you out there. Go find them.

Lydia opened her home to Paul. Her house became a real central part of Paul's operation in that area. These openings are out there for you.

GOD OPENS YOUR UNDERSTANDING

Ephesians 1:18 "The eyes of your understanding being enlightened; that ye may know..."

Jesus once said, *"It is given unto you to know the mysteries of the kingdom of God."* Believe this principle. You are the one to whom God gives an open mind.

The eyes of your understanding are being enlightened. You are beginning to know something about your position in the body of Christ. You are also beginning to operate as a Jesus man. This means you are successful.

You are wise.

You have favor.

You have power with God and with man.

You are in demand.

People want your services.

Luke 24:45 "Then opened he their understanding, that they might under-

stand the scriptures."

I see this happening in my life. I can see the Lord repeating this principle. He is teaching me to receive truths from His Word. He is giving me new messages for the body of Christ.

This is a principle of the spirit. He opened their understanding. He is opening my understanding more and more. I live by this principle. I anticipate this happening in my life. Praise His lovely name.

Psalm 119:18 "Open thou mine eyes, that I may behold wondrous things out of thy law."

God's Word is the way to successful living. This is not just knowing something about His Word. It is knowing how to be a success in life and to prepare oneself for eternity. It is being successful in blessing others that they may prosper and also inherit eternal life.

God is opening your eyes to opportunities daily. He is opening your eyes to what you need to see from His Word to develop your life. Look at His Word as exciting. God is personally speaking to you in it.

I get so excited when I read His Word. I often read it with a pen in hand. I read looking for something just for me. I may go through a chapter without writing anything down, or I may write two or three nuggets from each chapter. God speaks to you through His Word.

EXPECT THE HEAVENS
TO OPEN TO YOUR MINISTRY

Luke 3:21-22 "... Jesus also being baptized, and praying, the heaven was opened. And the Holy Ghost descended in a bodily shape like a dove upon him, and a voice came from heaven, which said, Thou art my beloved Son; in thee I am well pleased."

The Father wanted to confirm to the world the ministry of Jesus Christ. When He was baptized the Father did just that. Supernaturally God moved and confirmed that Jesus was and is His Son.

On several other occasions the Father demonstrated supernaturally with signs from heaven that Jesus was the Son of God.

Jesus Christ is in you. Your ministry is important. Expect God to confirm your ministry and your calling. It may not be as dramatic as it was when the Holy Spirit came upon Jesus in the form of a dove, but God will give you favor. He will have people favor and honor you. He will open doors for you. He will cause success to flow. He will make a way for people to recognize you and your contributions to this world. In many cases He will actually demonstrate in a little extra supernatural way that He has laid His hand upon you.

This is a law of the spirit. It will repeat itself in the lives of all who follow God. You will find this true throughout the Bible. It is true in your life. Expect it to happen.

Every time I start on a new phase of my ministry, God confirms it by prophecy or through conversations with godly people.

One time He spoke to me twice by prophecy concerning a certain phase. I responded by faith and began to take certain steps. The very next day another prophet who knew nothing of this came by and ministered to me in a very definite way confirming each phase of the operation. Then things began to fall in place more and more.

On another occasion my wife, Buddy, went to a service. Our ministry was just opening. Brother Haggin said, "Sister Buess, I see money coming through the air to you." This broke the financial pressure. From that day forward the doors of financial blessing opened for us.

GOD GIVES YOU A MOUTH OPEN WITH A MESSAGE

The world needs to hear you if you have something to say. Do you have a product that is good and needs to be sold? Believe that God gives you the opening of the mouth.

Do you have a personality that can be a blessing in business, churches, or other avenues? Believe that God gives you the opening of the mouth.

Do you have a ministry that would bless another? Believe that God gives you something to say that will please that interested party.

Ezekiel 29:21 "In that day I will cause the horn of the house of Israel to bud forth, and I will give thee the opening of the mouth in the midst of them..."

Ezekiel 33:22 "My mouth was opened, and I was no more dumb."

Spiritualizing this passage, the Lord will give to you the opening of the mouth. You will no longer be dumb (without words) in situations. God will give you words of wisdom to speak at the right time and in the right place. Visualize this happening to you. See wisdom flowing out of your mouth. Do not force these words. *"God will give you a mouth of wisdom..."* It will flow out at the right moment.

KNOCK THE DOORS OPEN BY PRAYER

Matthew 7:7-8 "Ask, and it shall be given you; seek, and ye shall find; knock, and it shall be opened unto you. For every one that asked receiveth; and he that seeketh findeth; and to him that knocketh it shall be opened."

If there is no response from simply asking, you might try hanging in there with a knock on heaven's door. If you do not get any response, you might try shaking the door a bit. God will not mind. Then, if you do not get any response, you might try kicking good and hard on the door. All of this is according to your own faith. Sometimes a little emotional release helps *your* faith. God's faith is all right.

Remember the story of the unjust judge and the widow lady in Luke 18:5,7-8. She wearied him by her continually coming to him. *"Because this widow troubleth me, I will avenge her, lest by her continual coming she weary me." "And shall not God avenge his own elect, which cry day and night unto him, though he bear long with them? I tell you that he will avenge them speedily..."*

Jesus said in Luke 16:16: *"... Every man presseth into it."* Press into the kingdom of God. Force your way into the kingdom. This is the reason I said you may have to rattle the door a bit and possibly even kick on it. The New American Standard Bible says of this passage, *"... Every one is forcing his way into it."*

For some men, doors open easily. For others every door seems to be nailed shut. If you will do some intense praying and positive confessing, it will help get things moving for you. Then get up and start applying pressure here and there. Soon you will find the key that unlocks those doors.

Business opportunities will begin to respond favorably to you. Financial situations will take on a different appearance. Everything will begin to respond to that faith pressure. God will honor your stepping out on the water with Jesus. Good things will happen.

OPEN YOUR EYES TO OPPORTUNITIES

Proverbs 20:13 "Love not sleep, lest thou come to poverty; open thine eyes, and thou shalt be satisfied with bread."

The power to produce is in you. *"I have come that they might have life, and that they might have it more abundantly."* (John 10:10)
Opportunities for success are in you.
Ideas for success are in you.
The kingdom of God is in you.

John 1:4 "In him was life; and the life was the light of men."

John 1:9 "That was the true Light, which lighteth every man that cometh into the world."

The life of Jesus is in you. It is in every man. When a man is born of the Spirit this life really comes alive. The world can use basic principles of the laws of God because they are made for man. A donkey cannot use them. He does not have this type of life. When a man is born of the Spirit these laws are more powerful. You need to use them.

"Love not sleep lest you come to poverty."

You could be working, but sleep calls you. Laziness calls. The ability is there, but the lazy spirit calls so loudly some just cannot respond to the success spirit and the call of Jesus Christ.

"Open thine eyes, and thou shalt be satisfied with bread."

The bread of success is yours. You must open your eyes and go after it.

CHAPTER 8

REIGNING BY PRAISING

Praising will not answer all of your questions nor solve all of your problems. At one time Paul sang and praised his way out of jail. On another occasion, he stayed in jail. I am sure he praised the time he was there, but the jail doors stayed closed.

Praise changes your attitude. It allows the Lord to move in your life and in the lives of others. It gives you strength to bear up in trials though the circumstances may seem just the same.

DEVELOP A MELODY IN YOUR HEART

Ephesians 5:19 ". . . Singing and making melody in your heart to the Lord."

Judges 5:3 ". . . I will sing unto the Lord; I will sing praise to the Lord God of Israel."

Psalm 7:17 ". . . I will sing praise to the

name of the Lord most high."

Psalm 57:7 "My heart is fixed, O God, my heart is fixed: I will sing and give praise."

Personally I love to sing the Psalms right out of my heart. I like to make my own melody as I go along. As I do this I hit a flow that works for me. It gives me a tremendous release.

I often sing and pray to the Lord using the Psalms as a springboard. Then I mix in lots of praise and worship.

You will find that you go and come with this type of worship.

I will do it often during the day for a week or so and then I leave it and move to another realm of praise and worship. I do not like to become hung up on any one type of praise or worship.

JESUS ALONE — THE OBJECT OF YOUR PRAISE

God is a jealous God. He wants your love and devotion. Learn to praise the Lord and not fleshly programs. Sometimes you hear a pastor or people in a certain church praising the name of their church. It does not take long to find who is the object of their praise. If you hear the church mentioned constantly instead of Jesus, it is easy to see that something is off center.

Jeremiah 17:14 ". . . Thou art my praise."

Psalm 22:25 "My praise shall be of thee in the great congregation..."

It is so much better to brag on Jesus than a church denomination. To make love to Jesus is so refreshing. It is absolutely honest. No man gets the glory.

The best thing you will ever do in this life is to develop a sincere love and praise to the Lord. Make love to Him and praise Him continually. He must be the object of your love and devotion and praise.

ABSENCE OF PRAISE SIGNIFIES DEATH

Psalm 30:11-12 "Thou hast turned for me my mourning into dancing: thou hast put off my sackcloth, and girded me with gladness; to the end that my glory may sing praise to thee, and not be silent..."

The silent spirit is the dead spirit. Mourning is death. Dancing is life. Gladness is life. The Lord has removed the sackcloth and mourning spirit and given you dancing feet and a dancing heart.

You may have to stir this up but it is there. The less you praise, the more death settles upon you.

Psalm 150:6 "Let every thing that hath breath praise the Lord..."

If you are still breathing, it is God's order to praise Him. Even a dog wags its tail.

Isaiah 38:18-19 "For the grave cannot

praise thee, death can not celebrate thee: they that go down into the pit cannot hope for thy truth. The living, the living, he shall praise thee..."

The dead man does not praise. He is silent. Religion without Jesus is like a graveyard. It is very dignified and silent. Where there is true life there is praise and thanksgiving. The lame man in Acts went leaping and praising. In Acts 8:8: *"There was great joy in the city."*

Demons were cast out.

People were healed.

People were saved.

Something great was happening, and there was joy. There was praise.

Psalm 115:17 "The dead praise not the Lord..."

Spiritually dead folks do not praise the Lord either.

PRAISE GLORIFIES THE LORD

Psalm 50:23 "Whoso offereth praise glorifieth me: and to him that ordereth his conversation aright will I shew the salvation of God."

A true praise glorifies and magnifies the Lord. If the Lord is lifted up, you too will be blessed. If the flesh is lifted up, you will eventually be drained. It is a question of praise and health, or lack of praise and ulcers.

Your entire conversation is to be one of

magnifying the Lord. You are to be positive and victorious. Murmuring in your "tents" is out. As you order your conversation aright, God begins to respond to this positive conversation. You get what you say. Good things begin to happen.

PRAISE BRINGS THE LORD INTO EACH SITUATION

Psalm 22:3 "But thou art holy, O thou that inhabitest the praise of Israel."

New American Standard Bible: *"Yet thou art holy, O thou who art enthroned upon the praises of Israel."*

Praise builds a throne for God. As you praise the Lord, you create an atmosphere which draws the real nature of God.

Unrest, murmuring, negativism, frustration, anger, and things of this nature drive God from the scene.

Praise, love, and adoration of the Lord regardless of the circumstance draw God there in full strength.

TEACH YOURSELF TO PRAISE THE LORD

2 Chronicles 23:13 ". . . Such as taught to sing praise . . ."

They had special people to lead out and to teach the congregation to sing and praise the Lord.

I once heard a man say that he did not want anyone to tell him when to praise. He said it should be spontaneous. If he felt like it, then he would praise the Lord.

No, sometimes you do not feel like it. You need to offer a "sacrifice of praise." They had special groups to teach them to praise. Your flesh becomes lazy and doesn't always want to praise. You need to be encouraged sometimes. You also need to teach yourself.

I did this. I did not feel like praising God so I worked on it continuously until I did feel like it.

Some people have come to me with the idea that they love to be quiet in their worship. They prefer a very soft praise or complete silence. There is a place for quiet praise. You should always have a praise in your heart. It is obvious that you will praise Him in a quiet spirit more often than any other type of praise.

It is not either/or in the case of praise. There is a time to shout for joy. There is a time to dance. There is a time for quietness. Learn to enjoy all the freedoms or moods set by the Holy Spirit. There were times in the scriptures where the noise of their shouts was heard at great distances.

PRAISE GOD CONTINUALLY

Psalm 34:1 "I will bless the Lord at all times: his praise shall continually be in my mouth."

The world worships Satan. His praise is

continually in their mouth.

You worship the Lord. His praise should continually be in your mouth.

I find it difficult to talk without praising and thanking the Lord at all times.

Psalm 71:6 ". . . My praise shall be continually of thee."

This is something that you need to work on constantly. If you really do not apply yourself there is a tendency to fall back into a rut of just praising now and then.

Luke 24:53 "And were continually in the temple, praising and blessing God."

This was the attitude of the New Testament church. They loved the Lord. They were still alive. Religion had not yet set in. They praised the Lord continually. Praise always accompanies a true revival.

If you are beginning to settle down to a lukewarm attitude toward praise, you can judge yourself. Religion is beginning to cheat you.

Perhaps you have never had a praise. Get one. You have been cheated. Praise is normal to true love and worship of the Father.

Psalm 71:8 "Let my mouth be filled with thy praise and with thy honour all the day."

Psalm 113:3 "From the rising of the sun unto the going down of the same the

Lord's name is to be praised."

Psalm 71:14 "... Will yet praise thee more and more."

Psalm 119:164 "Seven times a day do I praise thee because of thy righteous judgments."

Psalm 35:28 "And my tongue shall speak of thy righteousness and of thy praise all the day long."

Some of this praise is simply speaking or thinking about the Lord. It should come out in all of your thoughts. Perhaps you should not be projecting it too strongly in some conversations. The Holy Spirit will give you wisdom. Some folks can take more than others.

Run these scriptures by again.

"Let my mouth be filled with praise ... all the day."

"From the rising of the sun unto the going down of the same, the Lord's name is to be praised."

"... Will yet praise thee more and more."

"Seven times a day do I praise thee."

You are to praise Him all day long. You are to praise Him from the rising of the sun to the going down of the sun. On top of this you are to praise him more and more. Then seven times a day you are to praise him. This is approximately every two and a half hours of the time you are awake. Just let out a good blast of praise to clean out all of the worldly or fleshly carbon or static build up. It is good therapy.

Then if you still do not feel like praising the Lord, you are to *"Offer the sacrifice of praise to God continually, that is, the fruit of our lips giving thanks to his name."* (Hebrews 13:15)

Just slip up your hands right now and worship and love His lovely name.

As you do this just let every part of your being love and worship the Lord.

I did not used to praise the Lord. Now I praise Him often. When I received the baptism in the Holy Spirit I had been a minister for many years. I had a good faith experience but no great emotional release. My experience was real, but there was no great praise. Yes, there was a depth but that in itself is not enough.

I did not really enjoy pentecostals. I would visit with them after I received the Holy Ghost but I did not enjoy their freedom to worship and praise the Lord. I was in a strait betwixt the old church form and the worship of the pentecostals. Then on top of this I could detect that some of the pentecostals had some spirits that were not always the Lord. I recognized that I was missing something in spite of the foreign spirits intermingled. Sometimes I wanted to get back in my church. When I was in my church I wanted to get back in the pentecostal-type worship.

During this period of time I went with a pentecostal man to Mexico. We were in the car all day long. He blessed and praised the Lord all the day long too. I did not fully enjoy it. He was one of those men who had a few strange spirits mixed in with the Holy Ghost. Do not get excited about this. You too probably have some things strange to the Holy Ghost from time to time. Peter did when the Lord had to tell him, *"Get thee behind me, Satan."*

I was glad to get away from this brother so I could breathe freely and enjoy my form of silence before God. However, I was not satisfied that I was completely wrong or right. I decided to check the Word. I found the scriptures that I am sharing with you. I found that I was to praise Him continually. I was to praise Him from sunup to sundown. I found that I was to praise Him seven times a day. I was to offer a sacrifice of praise. Then on top of all of this, I was to praise Him more and more.

I decided to join them. I began to praise Him continually. I did this day and night. I would stay up deep into the night and praise the Lord. Or I would walk the living room praising the Lord. The family did not like it, but I had to get a breakthrough. I did this for thirty days before I began to enjoy it. My breakthrough came. From then on I found my praise. I enjoy my praise. I stirred up my praise. You need to do likewise if you have not yet done so. Praise Him till the release comes if it takes a year. Do it.

PRAISE HIM IN EVERYTHING

1 Thessalonians 5:18 "In everything give thanks: for this is the will of God in Christ Jesus concerning you."

You are to thank the Lord in everything but not for everything. You thank Him because He is bigger than your problem. He will help you through it. He is not responsible for many of your problems. Do not thank Him for something the devil did or something that you brought on that was not His will for you. You thank Him that He is still God. He still loves you. He is bringing you through. He is still God. He will turn everything around for good if you will form the right attitude.

Ephesians 5:20 "Giving thanks always for all things unto God and the Father in the name of our Lord Jesus Christ."

The Greek word translated "for" is *huper*. It is translated by Strong on page 74, Greek Dictionary no. 5228 as Over, above, beyond, across, for the sake of, instead, regarding, on the part of, for sake of, in stead, etc.*

---

*James Strong, *Strong's Exhaustive Concordance*, Compact Edition (Grand Rapids: Guardian Press), p.74.

In the Greek Lexicon by Abbott Smith the compound usage carries the idea of over or above.

In the light of all other teaching in the scripture it would only be fair to sound Bible translation to interpret this scripture, then, by thanking God over all things rather than for all things. Or you thank Him above all things rather than for all things. You move above the situation and praise the Lord.

You must not thank the Lord for the devil's work. You praise Him and go above the devil's work.

You cannot thank God that your child was murdered. You cannot thank God that your wife was raped. No. You go beyond it. You move above the situation and praise the Lord that He makes a way where there seemeth to be no way.

Romans 8:28 "We know that all things work together for good to them that love God..."

God is able to turn it around and get good out of what the devil meant for evil. So you can praise the Lord in all things but not for all things. Praise ye the Lord.

James 1:2 "My brethren, count it all joy when ye fall into divers temptations."

We have learned to praise the Lord when pressures hit. Lillian (Buddy) and I do not always feel like it, but we do it anyway. We may fuss a little, but we have developed the idea of praising more than fussing.

1 Peter 4:12-13 "Beloved, think it not strange concerning the fiery trial which is to try you . . . but rejoice, inasmuch as ye are partakers of Christ's sufferings . . ."

When demonic pressures hit, shout your way through. If you are guilty of something, talk to the Lord about it. Get it out of your system. Do not leave Satan on your back. He will take undue advantage of you. Move right into praise and worship. This will wash your system clean of all guilt and all demonic pressures. God's way is always best.

Habakkuk 3:17-18 "Although the fig tree shall not blossom, neither shall fruit be in the vines; the labour of the olive shall fail, and the fields shall yield no meat; the flock shall be cut off from the fold, and there shall be no herd in the stalls: Yet I will rejoice in the Lord, I will joy in the God of my salvation."

The prophet made a strong confession in these scriptures. He said if everything went sour, he would still rejoice. If he lost his job, so to speak, he would still praise the Lord. If there was a severe drought, he would still praise the Lord. If the food and water were down to nothing, he would still praise God. How could he do this? He answers this with the following scripture.

Habakkuk 3:19 "The Lord God is my strength, and he will make my feet like hinds' feet, and he will make me to walk upon mine high places."

He said, *"God is my source."* This was the essence of his confession. If things go bad, rejoice. God is your source. If you lose your job, praise the Lord for a better one. If you lost it due to your negligence, correct your error and praise God for His love and mercy and get a better job.

One man who taught on praise quite often found himself in a dilemma. He had two flat tires and no spare. He began to fuss and fume. He was under pressure and frustration was taking over. His wife told him that he had better praise the Lord if he expected to get help. He fussed back at her and told her to shut up. After another long period of time his wife reminded him that he had taught folks to praise in everything and that he might practice what he had been preaching. He finally simmered down and began to praise the Lord. Within a very short period of time a man stopped by in a pick-up. He had two tires already mounted in the back of the truck. This stranger changed the flat tires for his new tires. He did not even take them off the wheels. He just mounted the new tires and wheels on the preacher's car. Then he left. The preacher did not even get his name. He did not charge him for them. To this day the minister feels like this might have been an angel. Whether it was or not, we may never know. One thing for sure, he was an angel to this needy man.

Learn to shift above your problem and praise the Lord. If you have trouble with personalities, husband, wife, or neighbors, turn the love and compassion of Jesus loose. Look at the situation through the eyes of Jesus and begin to praise. If there is something you can do in the natural to relieve the situation, do it. But continue in the attitude of praise and victory. See beyond the problem. See the glory of God moving on your behalf.

Take a look right now at life. Get the frown off your face. See Jesus clearing out the snowbanks.

Philippians 4:4 "Rejoice in the Lord always: and again I say, rejoice."

Joy and praise are more powerful than the negative forces. As you rejoice, regardless of circumstances, you are calling on God to release the pressure. You are entering into the positive aspect of God.

Luke 6:22-23 "Blessed are ye, when men shall hate you, and when they shall separate you from their company, and shall reproach you, and cast out your name as evil, for the Son of man's sake.

Rejoice ye in that day, and leap for joy..."

Try leaping for joy. Break the stiff-neck spirit. I did this fifteen minutes a day for two weeks until I began to rejoice as I leaped for joy. When pressures hit, get alone with God and literally begin to leap for joy. Sooner or later you will see joy fill your soul. Love will flow instead of irritation. If someone has mistreated you, love will fill your heart for that person.

If you are like I used to be, leaping for joy will not help you much at first. That is why I did it for two weeks straight for fifteen minutes a day. Now when I begin to rejoice and praise the Lord, joy floods my soul immediately. It is super. Praise His lovely name.

PRAISE BRINGS THE VICTORY

Psalm 106:47 "...Triumph in thy praise."

You overcome the enemy that has come against you by worship and praise. Much is said in the scriptures about *"murmuring in the tents."* The troubled spirit breeds more trouble. You reap what you sow. The victory spirit breeds more victory.

2 Chronicles 20:22 "When they began to sing and to praise, the Lord set ambushments against the children of Ammon, Moab, and mount Seir, which were

come against Judah; and they were smitten."

Judah means praise. They decided to have a victory praise meeting before they went to battle. The enemy was coming up the mountain so they wanted to prepare for their encounter with him by praise. *"He appointed singers unto the Lord, and that should praise the beauty of holiness, as they went before the army, and to say, Praise the Lord..."*

Praise stopped the enemy. Strife broke out in the enemy camp. Civil war took over. They killed each other. Judah, the praisers, did not have to fight. They spent three days in gathering the riches from the dead bodies of the enemy. They could not carry it all.

You may have to become actively engaged in problems from time to time. There were other times when they had to go to battle, but God helped them in the battle.

The walls of Jerico fell when the people gave a big shout.

Joshua 6:20 "... The people shouted with a great shout, that the wall fell down flat..."

Practice shouting your walls down rather than fussing at them.

Acts 16:25-26 "And at midnight Paul and Silas prayed, and sang praises unto God; and the prisoners heard them. And suddenly there was a great earthquake, so

that the foundations of the prison were shaken: and immediately all the doors were opened, and every one's bands were loosed."

Praise was so powerful in this case that supernatural deliverance took place. The prison was shaken. The bands were loosed from all the prisoners. The jailer and his household were converted. Paul was loosed the next day officially.

Praise will do this for you. Perhaps not so dramatically, but God will move. I should say that you cannot use praise as a legalistic way of telling God how to operate. Paul later was thrown in jail and remained there for years. He still praised the Lord.

Proverbs 15:15 ". . . He that is of a merry heart hath a continual feast."

Proverbs 17:22 "A merry heart doeth good like a medicine: but a broken spirit drieth the bones."

Nehemiah 8:10 ". . . Neither be ye sorry; for the joy of the Lord is your strength."

Isaiah 12:3 ". . . With joy shall ye draw water out of the wells of salvation."

If you want a continual feast, learn to develop a merry heart. Visualize yourself as a happy and joyful person.

The joy of the Lord creates strength. Visualize your life as a generator that praises and rejoices through to healthy situations.

A merry heart is like a medicine in your life. An attitude of praise and joy brings healing. An attitude of sorrow brings bad health. It drieth the bones.

"With joy shall ye draw water."

From a normal well you draw water with a rope and bucket or a pump. From the well of salvation you draw water with joy. Joy draws living water to you. The more you rejoice the more living waters flow from the well of salvation to you. Try it. You will like it.

BOOKS BY BOB BUESS

King David and I	1.95
High Flight	1.95
Implanted Word	1.95
The Race Horse	1.25
Discipleship Pro and Con	1.95
The Pendulum Swings	1.95
The Laws of the Spirit	1.50
Setting the Captives Free	1.50
Deliverance From the Bondage of Fear	1.50
Favor, the Road to Success	1.25
You Can Receive the Holy Ghost Today	1.50
Confession Pack (Scripture cards)	1.00

All 12 of the above for $15.00 including postage. This is a $20.00 value for only $15.00!

When ordering up to 3 books include 60¢ postage. Add 20¢ for each additional 3 books or fraction thereof.

Texas residents please include 4% sales tax unless you are qualified for tax exemption.

In orders of 30 books or more, you may deduct 35%.

Please add postage and sales tax on discounted total, if applicable.

Bookstores and jobbers receive other discounts.

No discounts when ordering at the special set prices.

King David's throne is prophetic for the church.

Victories won by King David represent your victories in Christ.

King David's anointing was passed on to his men who were able to do exploits.

Jesus Christ, our King David, passes his anointing on to you, and you too can do exploits.

King Solomon is an extension of David's throne. Wisdom operates on David's throne. The true wisdom is found in Jesus. This is the believer's inheritance. Claim your wisdom by faith just as you do healing.

There was much wealth on David's throne. This was also manifested in Solomon's kingdom. Jesus Christ our David gives us all things to enjoy. All the money you will ever need for your ministry on earth is provided in Jesus.

King David was famous. Jesus was famous. Jesus in you is famous. Claim this fame for the body of Christ. Claim this fame for your own ministry and then hold your confession. Work it out in your life.

King David's throne was one of joy as he danced before the Lord. Jesus was anointed with joy above his fellows. You are on a joy throne.

Form a picture in your mind of a throne with you sitting there with Jesus. Let this picture of your throne bring you through your problems.